WALKING

WASHINGTON, D.C.

WALKING
WASHINGTON, D.C.

THE BEST OF THE CITY

Barbara Noe Kennedy

Photography by Lisa A. Walker

NATIONAL GEOGRAPHIC

Washington, D.C.

WALKING
WASHINGTON, D.C.

CONTENTS

PART 1

PAGE 12
WHIRLWIND TOURS

PART 2

PAGE 42
WASHINGTON'S NEIGHBORHOODS

PART 3

PAGE 176
TRAVEL ESSENTIALS

**Previous pages:
Jefferson Memorial;
opposite: strolling
the Penn Quarter;
right: bust of George
Washington, National
Portrait Gallery;
top right: view from
POV bar; bottom
right: World War II
Memorial**

Introduction

Everyone owns the National Mall, but no one ever offers to mow it. That's Washington, D.C., a city built on compromise and still bristling under the arrangement. When the capital district was sited here in 1790, this partial swamp was intended to bring a southerly sensibility to the nation's northern economic center. It's hard to say if that worked. John F. Kennedy quipped: "Washington is a city of southern efficiency and northern charm." D.C. is a city of such symbolic magnitude and structural presence that the people who live here, and the qualities that make us unique, are often obscured. The oddest thing to say about the nation's capital is that it's "a city of transients." What city worth its salt isn't? Any other city with this sort of turnover would be celebrated as a hotbed of reinvention. And that's exactly what Washington is today. A buzzing hub of interconnected neighborhoods (pedal a Capital Bikeshare cycle from Logan Circle to Shaw). A community of hungry explorers (feast up 14th Street N.W. or devour Union Market) with a spirit for invention (the gin rickey was first stirred in D.C.). A creative and globalized set of brainy bureaucrats and socialized millennials who love their local brew (Compass Coffee is tops, DC Brau is hops). But here's a concession we can all agree on: Washington is not an "either/or" city. It's a "both/and" kind of town. So get your walking shoes on and go explore the District of Columbia with an uncompromising sense of discovery.

The oddest thing to say about the nation's capital is that it's "a city of transients." What city worth its salt isn't?

George W. Stone
Editor in Chief, National Geographic Traveler *magazine*

Visiting Washington, D.C.

A noble capital glowing with marble monuments, Washington, D.C., offers public parks, more than 50 museums (many with free admission), and year-round cultural events. But gridlock can snarl travelers as well as politicians. Here are some tips.

Washington in a Nutshell

The Father of the Country, George Washington himself, selected an unlikely, undeveloped spot on the Potomac River to build the nation's capital—the result of a compromise between the northern and southern states. French architect Pierre-Charles L'Enfant designed the Capital City, giving it a European flair centered around a grand esplanade—the National Mall—lined by the most important government buildings. From here, distinct neighborhoods fan out into a quadrant of districts (see sidebar opposite), home today to some 650,000 residents.

Visiting the Sights

Many sights have security measures in place, including bag checks and metal detectors. Entry to museums may be long during peak seasons and holidays. Be sure to pack for the day wisely to assist in getting through the line quickly; also, note that some sights prohibit

Washington, D.C., Day by Day

Open every day (with some exceptions for major holidays) All Smithsonian museums, including National Zoo; National Gallery of Art; monuments; and most government buildings.

Monday Many sights are closed, including the African American Civil War Museum, Anderson House, Carlyle House Historic Park, Dumbarton House, Dumbarton Oaks, Eastern Market, Gadsby's Tavern Museum *(Nov.–March)*, Lee-Fendall House, Phillips Collection, President Woodrow Wilson House, Octagon House, Stabler-Leadbeater Apothecary Museum *(Nov.–March)*, and Tudor Place Historic House & Garden.

Tuesday Sights closed include Decatur House, Gadsby's Tavern Museum *(Nov.–March)*, Lee-Fendall House, Octagon House, and Stabler-Leadbeater Apothecary Museum *(Nov.–March)*.

Wednesday Octagon House is closed.

Thursday Decatur House is closed.

Friday All major sights are open!

Sat.–Sun. Most museums in the Capital City are open weekends. However Decatur House and the U.S. Supreme Court are closed. Octagon House is open Sat. but closed Sun.

Waves of shadow and refracted light infuse this courtyard shared by the Smithsonian American Art Museum and the National Portrait Gallery.

certain items, such as water bottles, sharp objects, etc. The White House is especially strict. Check websites ahead of time for more specific information.

In many places, including Ford's Theatre, Washington Monument, and National Archives, you can skip long lines if you preorder timed passes online for a small fee.

Be aware that some sights can only be visited by guided tour, at specific times. The itineraries in this book aim to accommodate such restrictions, but keep them in mind as you plan your tour of the places you most want to explore. Also, many attractions offer insightful guided interpretive tours, lectures, IMAX movies, and other

intriguing programs throughout the day. Check websites or call ahead of time to make the most of your visit to the Capital City.

IN **THE KNOW**

The city is laid out in four quadrants, with the Capitol building in the center. North Capitol, South Capitol, and East Capitol Streets radiate from here, separating the city into quadrants (the Mall runs west from the Capitol building). So, when seeking a sight, first check the quadrant address, which indicates where it lies— N.W., N.E., S.W., or S.E.? Be advised that many addresses can be found in more than one quadrant (for instance, there is a 4000 M St. in N.E., S.E., S.W., and N.W.—four different D.C. locations).

Using This Guide

Each tour—which might be only a walk, or might also take advantage of the city's public transportation—is plotted on a map and has been planned to take into account opening hours and the times of day when sights are less crowded. Many end near restaurants or lively nightspots for evening activities.

Whirlwind Tours

Whirlwind Tours are for people who have only a day or a weekend to spend in the city and want to ensure that they see the best of the best. Choose your tour based on your available time and interests: One Day, Two Days, For Fun, With Kids, African-American Heritage, and Embassy Row.

Tips For the One-Day and Two-Day Tours, a Tips spread following each itinerary map provides insider information on detours from the key sights, extra places to see, nearby restaurants, and ideas for adapting the tours to suit your interests.

Sight Descriptions

In the Whirlwind Tours, key sights spreads following the maps provide descriptions of all the sights and practical information for visitors.

Neighborhood Tours

The seven neighborhood tours each begin with an introduction, followed by an itinerary map highlighting the key sights that make up the tour plus detailed key sight descriptions. Each tour is followed by an "in-depth" spread showcasing one major sight along the route, a "distinctly D.C." spread providing background information on a quintessential element that relates to that neighborhood, and a "best of" spread that groups sights thematically.

Itinerary Map A map of the neighborhood shows the locations of the key sights, Metro stations, and main streets.

Captions These captions briefly describe the key sights and give instructions on finding the next stop on the tour. Full descriptions of the sights may be found on the following pages.

Route
Dotted lines link the key sights.

Price Ranges for Key Sites

$	$1–$5
$$	$6–$10
$$$	$11–$15
$$$$	$16–$20
$$$$$	$21+

Price Ranges for Good Eats
(for one person, excluding drinks)

$	Under $10
$$	$11–$20
$$$	$21–$35
$$$$	$36–$50
$$$$$	$51+

Key Sights Descriptions These spreads provide a detailed description and highlights for each sight, following the order on the map, plus each one's address, phone number, website, entrance fee, days closed, and nearest Metro station.

Good Eats Refer to these lists for a selection of locally recommended restaurants and cafés along the route.

Kayakers on the Potomac River, beneath
the Francis Scott Key Bridge

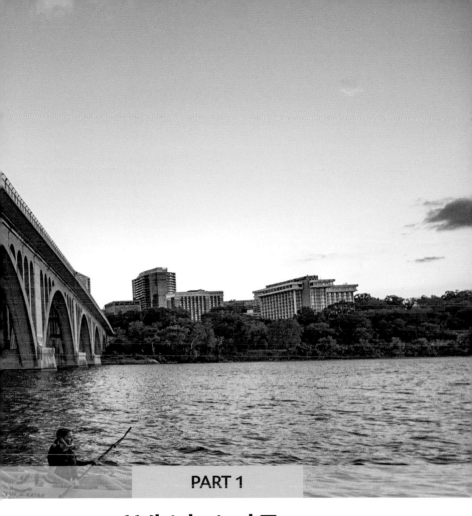

PART 1

Whirlwind Tours

D.C. in a Day

*Experience Washington's most popular sights
on this packed, one-day tour.*

Georgetown

M STREET

Chesapeake & Ohio Canal

PENNSYLVANIA AVE

29

FOGGY
BOTTOM

I ST. N.W.

GEORGETOWN
WATERFRONT
PARK

66

Foggy
Bottom—
GWU

H ST.

Potomac

G ST.

22ND ST.

21ST ST.

20TH ST.

19TH ST.

18TH ST.

F ST.

66

VIRGINIA

E ST.

Kennedy
Center

23RD STREET N.W.

Department
of State

D ST.

C ST.

22ND ST.

20TH ST.

17TH ST.

5 Georgetown (see pp. 142–151)
Grab dinner at a stylish restaurant and, if
you have extra time, poke into some of the
city's poshest boutiques. Walk about a mile
(1.6 km) to the Kennedy Center via paths
alongside the Potomac—or take a cab.

Farragut
West

McPherson
Square

H ST.

LAFAYETTE
SQUARE

**White
House**

NEW YORK AVE.

E ST.

D ST.

C ST.

THE
ELLIPSE

CONSTITUTION AVENUE

50

Vietnam
Veterans
Memorial

CONSTITUTION
GARDENS

**Monuments
& Memorials**

N.W.
S.W.

Lincoln
Memorial

Reflecting Pool

WEST POTOMAC PARK

National
WWII
Memorial

Washington
Monument

Korean War
Veterans Memorial

D.C. War
Memorial

KUTZ BRIDGE

INDEPENDENCE AVE.

OHIO DRIVE

WEST BASIN DRIVE

*Tidal
Basin*

6 Kennedy Center (see p. 17)
Finish your day with a dazzling
show—ballet, symphony, opera,
or theater—at this legendary
cultural center.

Franklin Delano
Roosevelt
Memorial

Jefferson
Memorial

0   200 meters
0   200 yards

D.C. IN A DAY   DISTANCE: 7.5 MILES (12 KM)
TIME: 16 HOURS   METRO: SMITHSONIAN

❹ Capitol Hill (see pp. 68–77) Swing past the U.S. Capitol, Library of Congress, and the U.S. Supreme Court then head to Union Station where you can hop on the Circulator bus (or take a cab) to Georgetown, about 5.5 miles (9 km) away.

❸ National Air & Space Museum
(see pp. 60–63) Applaud triumphs in air and space at the nation's most visited museum. Exiting onto Independence Ave., S.W., turn left; go up the hill to First St., S.E., and turn left.

❶ Monuments & Memorials
(see pp. 46–55) Celebrate democracy on an early morning stroll. Then head north a few blocks to the White House at 1600 Pennsylvania Ave., N.W.

❷ White House
(see pp. 118–121) See where P.O.T.U.S. lives, works, and entertains. Go south on 15th St., N.W., to the Mall and turn left on Jefferson Dr., S.W., to 7th St., S.W.

Tips

There's a lot to cover in Washington, D.C.—really too much for just one day! That said, this tour jam-packs the biggest and the best the Capital City has to offer, beginning at the National Mall and fanning out from there.

❶ Monuments & Memorials

(see pp. 46–55) The monuments and memorials to the west of the National Mall are open 24 hours a day; if you arrive early, you're likely to have them to yourself. The most stunning views are from the steps of the Lincoln Memorial looking east toward the sunrise, the Washington Monument, and the U.S. Capitol. Beginning your day at the ■ WASHINGTON MONU-MENT, a 2-mile (3 km) walk takes in the ■ NATIONAL WORLD WAR II MEMORIAL, ■ VIETNAM VETERANS MEMORIAL, ■ LINCOLN MEMORIAL, ■ MARTIN LUTHER KING, JR. MEMO-RIAL, ■ FDR MEMORIAL, and ■ THOMAS JEFFERSON MEMORIAL—all before the rest of town has had a cup of coffee.

❷ White House (see pp. 118–121)

Even if you don't have tickets to tour the President's House, there are other experiences to be had. You can admire the White House from all sides and angles by following the exterior gate all around, first along Pennsylvania Avenue, then along the Ellipse (see if you can pick out the sharp-shooters on the roof). Or rest on a park bench in ■ LAFAYETTE SQUARE, just across Pennsylvania Avenue, and gaze at the White House from afar. You can also visit a lesser known presidential residence, the ■ OCTAGON HOUSE (see p. 114), just a block away. A good choice for brunch nearby is the ■ HAMILTON (600 14th St., N.W., tel 202-787-1000, thehamiltondc.com), a buzzing dining and entertainment venue in the former Garfinckel's department store. Come back in the evening for a live concert.

❸ National Air & Space Museum (see pp. 60–63) This

popular Smithsonian museum has extended hours on certain dates (a great time to go, when the crowds have thinned)—check website for details.

4 Capitol Hill (see pp. 68–77)
The major sights on "the Hill" line up along First Street, where the city's northeast and southeast quadrants align: the ■ **U.S. Capitol** (see pp. 78–81), the ■ **Library of Congress's Thomas Jefferson Building** (see pp. 72–73), and the ■ **U.S. Supreme Court** (see pp. 74–75). If you want to tour the Capitol but haven't reserved tickets through your congressperson in advance, check if any of the first-come, first-served tickets are still available at the U.S. Capitol Visitor Center's lower level. Here you can also pop into ■ **Emancipation Hall,** offering well-curated exhibits, original documents, videos, and an interesting cross section model of the Capitol dome.

5 Georgetown (see pp. 142–151)
This fun neighborhood's main shopping streets are M Street, N.W., between 29th and 35th Streets and Wisconsin Avenue, N.W., north of M Street. The ■ **Chesapeake & Ohio Canal** (*tel 301-739-4200, nps.gov/ choh*) offers a scenic stroll along the historic waterway's towpath; the most charming section is between Thomas Jefferson Street and 31st Street, N.W. Or sit on a bench at ■ **Georgetown Waterfront Park** and enjoy watching D.C.'s movers and shakers at play

CUSTOMIZING **YOUR DAY**

The long National Mall, plus the miles of hallways awaiting inside each of the major museums, will test your walking stamina. Do your feet a favor by buying a ticket for a hop-on hop-off bus, which allows you to get on and off at popular stops. Big Bus Tours *(bigbustours.com)* and CitySights DC *(citysightsdc.com)* are among those offering this service.

with the Potomac as a backdrop. Stop at D.C. classic ■ **Clyde's of George-town** *(3236 M St., N.W., tel 202-333-9180)* to enjoy a pre-theater meal.

6 Kennedy Center Take a free guided tour of this performing arts center, a "national living memorial" to the 35th president, or just wander beneath the flags of the ■ **Hall of States** and ■ **Hall of Nations.** Better still, catch a show at one of the many theaters; the ■ **Millennium Stage** *(kennedy-center.org)* has free shows at 6 p.m. most evenings. Need dinner? The Roof Terrace Restaurant *(tel 202-416-8555)*, or the casual KC Café are options. You can even preorder an intermission snack or drink by printing out the online form and handing it to a bartender when you arrive. And be sure to walk out on the balcony for lovely views over the Potomac.

WHIRLWIND TOURS

DAY
1

D.C. in Two Days

Day One of a two-day tour takes in the National Mall followed by shopping in Georgetown and a show at the Kennedy Center

❼ Georgetown (see pp. 142–151) Shop and dine in one of the city's poshest neighborhoods. Then walk about a mile (1.6 km) to the Kennedy Center, via pathways alongside the Potomac—or take a cab.

❻ Arlington National Cemetery (see p. 21) Pay homage to the soldiers who made the greatest sacrifice in conflicts as far back as the Civil War. When you're ready, walk about a mile (1.6 km) through Rosslyn and across Key Bridge to Georgetown, or take the Metro's blue line one stop to the Rosslyn station and walk across Key Bridge—or take a cab.

❽ Kennedy Center (see p. 17) Cap your day with a spectacular show at this venerable cultural center on the Potomac.

WHIRLWIND TOURS

D.C. IN TWO DAYS DISTANCE: 7 MILES (11 KM)
TIME: APPROX. 16 HOURS METRO: SMITHSONIAN

❶ National Mall (see pp. 46–57) Take an early morning stroll around the National Mall's monuments, then head north to the White House, 1600 Pennsylvania Ave., N.W.

❷ White House (see pp. 118–121) Explore the president's home (if you have reservations) or hit the nearby White House Visitor Center. Then go back to the Mall, and turn left on Madison Dr., N.W.

❸ National Museum of American History (see pp. 58–59) Seek out Dorothy's ruby slippers and other cultural icons at this repository. Continue east along the Mall.

❹ National Gallery of Art (see pp. 56–57) Take your pick: Byzantine altarpieces and French Impressionists in the West Building, or pop art and modern mobiles in the East Building. Or both. Then walk across to the other side of the Mall.

❺ National Air & Space Museum (see pp. 60–63) See the very vehicles that transported humankind from the aviation age into the space age. Then take the Metro's blue line from the Smithsonian station to the Arlington Cemetery station.

Tips

Two days give you a little more time to get to know this beautiful city.

Spend Day One on the National Mall, with entertaining diversions to

Georgetown and the Kennedy Center. Here are some tips to get you going,

along with some possible alternatives to customize your visit.

WHIRLWIND TOURS

DAY 1

❷ **White House** (see pp. 118–121)
Spend time at the ■ WHITE HOUSE
VISITOR CENTER for fascinating
insights into life at the White House
past and present. If the nation's early
history interests you, walk to the
nearby ■ OCTAGON HOUSE (see p.
114), which served as the presidential
residence for James Madison for a
brief time after the British burned
Washington in 1814. Another good
option for history buffs is ■ DECATUR
HOUSE on Lafayette Square (see pp.
111–112), home to the War of 1812
hero. Tour hours are limited, but beautifully curated special exhibitions in
their parlor rooms offer another way
to get a glimpse into early Washington.
Check the website for what's on show.

❸ **National Museum of American History** (see p. 58–59) The
museum's docent-led highlights tours

are an enjoyable way to make sure
you hit the must-see sights in a short
amount of time. And even if your
packed schedule doesn't allow for a
full visit to the fascinating ■ NATIONAL
MUSEUM OF NATURAL HISTORY (see
p. 56) next door, at the very least
poke your head inside to admire the
■ AFRICAN BUSH ELEPHANT and the
fabled ■ HOPE DIAMOND. For a breath
of fresh air, the adjacent ■ BUTTERFLY
HABITAT GARDEN (gardens.si.edu)
draws butterflies to the urban setting.
Nearby, the brand-new (2016)
■ NATIONAL MUSEUM OF AFRICAN
AMERICAN HISTORY AND CULTURE
(see p. 36) tells the story of the United
States from the African-American
point of view. Across the National
Mall, the iconic turreted ■ CASTLE
(see sidebar p. 51) shows off a selection
of fascinating objects from many of
the Smithsonian's 19 area museums;
enjoy a short film and a coffee, too.

❹ National Gallery of Art

(see pp. 56–57) Start at the front desk, where a "highlights" tour brochure pinpoints the most famous works in both buildings (they also have one for kids). If you are an art devotee, take one of the informative docent-led tours. Outside, the ■ NATIONAL GALLERY OF ART SCULPTURE GARDEN *(6th St. & Constitution Ave., N.W., tel 202-737-4215, nga.gov)* is an interesting stop for the whole family, with its larger-than-life installations (starring Claes Oldenburg and Joan Miró) and jazz concerts on summer Fridays; in winter its fountain transforms into a skating rink. If time allows, other fascinating museums on the Mall are the ■ FREER GALLERY OF ART and the ■ ARTHUR M. SACKLER GALLERY *(asia .si.edu)*, both devoted to Asian art; the ■ NATIONAL MUSEUM OF AFRICAN ART *(africa.si.edu)*; the curving ■ NATIONAL

National Museum of the American Indian

CUSTOMIZING **YOUR DAY**

The Smithsonian offers all kinds of fun goings-on, including festivals, films, talks, workshops, and shows—most for free. One of the most popular summer events is **Asia After Dark** at the Freer and Sackler Galleries, a night of tours, Bollywood-inspired dance classes, music, and specialty cocktails. **Cooking Up History** at the National Museum of American History dishes up the story behind favorite American foods with a guest chef in the on-site demonstration kitchen. Check *si.edu* for more offerings.

MUSEUM OF THE AMERICAN INDIAN *(nmai.si.edu)*; and the ■ HIRSHHORN MUSEUM AND SCULPTURE GARDEN *(hirshhorn.si.edu)*, showcasing contemporary art and culture. Remember, they're all free!

❻ Arlington National Cemetery

After absorbing the sobering rows of white headstones, take in the ceremonial ■ CHANGING OF THE GUARD AT THE TOMB OF THE UNKNOWNS, the moving ■ ETERNAL FLAME at John F. Kennedy's grave, and Robert E. Lee's graceful mansion, ■ ARLINGTON HOUSE. A pathway outside the cemetery entrance winds north to the nearby ■ IWO JIMA MEMORIAL, at the end of Memorial Bridge *(arlington cemetery.mil; Metro: Arlington Cemetery)*.

DAY
2

D.C. in Two Days

Explore Capitol Hill, a trendy new quarter, a classic restaurant beloved by political insiders, and a show at an award-winning regional theater on the second day of your two-day tour.

5 **Penn Quarter** (see pp. 90–95) Find refreshment at one of this buzzing neighborhood's hip cafés near the Verizon Center, then visit your choice of several top-notch museums, such as the Newseum. Go west on F St., N.W., to 15th St., N.W., and turn right to the corner of G St., N.W.

6 **Old Ebbitt Grill** (see p. 85) Come dinnertime, keep an eye out for White House staffers as you dig into oysters at this legendary eatery. Take the Metro's red or green line from the Metro Center station to the Waterfront station and walk a block.

7 **Arena Stage** (see p. 25) Round out your day with a show at this famous regional theater.

D.C. IN TWO DAYS   DISTANCE: 3.25 MILES (5.2 KM)
TIME: APPROX. 15 HOURS   METRO: EASTERN MARKET

4 U.S. Supreme Court (see pp. 74–75) Pay homage to the highest court in the land. Go north one block to Constitution Ave., N.E., turn left, and walk to 7th St., N.W., turning right to reach the vicinity of F St., N.W.

3 Library of Congress (see pp. 72–73) Visit the dazzling neoclassical Thomas Jefferson Building, full of statues, columns, and frescoes—but where are the books? You'll find out. Go north, next door to 1st St., N.E.

5 Penn Quarter

Archives–Navy Memorial

C ST.

AVENUE

7TH ST.

6TH ST.

MADISON DRIVE NW

3RD ST. NW

CONSTITUTION AVE.

LOUISIANA AVE.

MALL

JEFFERSON DRIVE SW

4TH ST.

Capitol Reflecting Pool

Northwest **Northeast**

Southwest **Southeast**

4 U.S. Supreme Court

3 Library of Congress

U.S. Botanic Garden

U.S. Capitol

INDEPENDENCE AVE.

CAPITOL HILL

FIRST ST. SE.

2ND ST. SE.

A ST. S.E.

Eastern Market 1

C ST. S.E.

7TH ST. S.E.

PENNSYLVANIA AVE.

L'Enfant Plaza

MARYLAND AVE.

C ST.

Federal Center S.W.

VIRGINIA AVE

E ST.

Eastern Market

7TH ST.

6TH ST.

4TH ST.

G ST.

I ST SW

SOUTHWEST WATERFRONT

Arena Stage **7**

Waterfront Metro

M ST. S.W.

7 U.S. Capitol (see pp. 78–81) See the famous Rotunda and National Statuary Hall, and, if Congress is in session, watch politicians in action on the gallery floor. Then find the underground tunnel to the Library of Congress.

1 Eastern Market (see pp. 76–77) Take the blue line Metro from downtown and rub elbows with locals over blueberry buckwheat pancakes at Eastern Market. Then follow 7th St., S.E., north to E. Capitol St., N.E., and the Capitol.

WHIRLWIND TOURS

Tips

Day Two of your two-day tour begins on Capitol Hill, where you can mix some local flavor with important national sites. Next explore the trendy Penn Quarter neighborhood with its happening restaurants and museums, dine at an iconic D.C. restaurant, and finish your day at an award-winning regional theater.

WHIRLWIND TOURS

DAY 2

❶ Eastern Market (see pp. 76–77) In addition to those at the popular Eastern Market, breakfast options on the Hill include local favorites ■ PETE'S DINER at 212 2nd St., S.E. *(tel 202-544-7335)* and ■ JIMMY T'S PLACE at 501 E. Capitol St., S.E. *(tel 202-546-3646).*

❷ U.S. Capitol (see pp. 78–81) If there's no time for a tour, at least visit the U.S. Capitol Visitor Center's insightful, exhibit-filled ■ EMANCIPATION HALL. Get there early before the crowds begin, since you will have to stand in line for security. A stroll all around this giant classical edifice is enjoyable as well—go down the Capitol's south side along Independence Avenue to the lush greenhouses of the ■ U.S. BOTANIC GARDEN (see p. 156); then cross the front facade by the ■ CAPITOL REFLECTING POOL before climbing back up the Capitol's other

side. You'll come across pocket gardens, hidden statues, and plenty of benches.

❸ Library of Congress (see pp. 72–73) The one-hour tour of this over-the-top beaux arts temple to books provides a great behind-the-scenes look at the library's history and design. Otherwise, pick up a self-guided tour brochure and find your way to the stunning ■ GREAT HALL and ■ MAIN READING ROOM.

❹ U.S. Supreme Court (see pp. 74–75) Want to see an oral argument at the nation's highest court, but don't want to spend the time standing in line? Hire a line stander! Seating for the first oral argument begins at 9:30 a.m.; to assure a seat, your line stander should be there at least 12 hours ahead of time. Search online for "DC line standing." The current rate is about $50 per hour.

❺ Penn Quarter (see pp. 90–95)
Grab a bite at one of the many trendy downtown restaurants, then spend the afternoon in one of the area's fabulous museums. Art lovers should head straight to the ■ SMITHSONIAN AMERICAN ART MUSEUM (see pp. 93–94); newshounds (and anyone captivated by history) should devote plenty of time to the ■ NEWSEUM (see pp. 96–99); and lovers of intrigue should go to the ■ INTERNATIONAL SPY MUSEUM (see pp. 94–95). If you don't tarry, you'll have time for quick visits to at least two of the three. For food, ■ CLYDE'S OF GALLERY PLACE (707 7th St., N.W., tel 202-349-3700), ■ DISTRICT TACO (1309 F St., N.W., tel 202-347-7359), and ■ JALEO (480 7th St., N.W., tel 202-628-7949) are fun options.

❻ Old Ebbitt Grill (see p. 85)
Presidents Grant, Cleveland, Harding, and Theodore Roosevelt all hung out at this upscale, Victorian-style saloon, and today you still might spot a political insider or two. T. R. himself is said to have captured the walrus hanging at the bar. Seeking something a little more mod? The nearby ■ POV (see p. 84) rooftop bar at the hotel W Washington D.C. has cushioned sofas and great views. More restaurants are to the east, between 7th and 14th Sts., N.W.

CUSTOMIZING **YOUR DAY**

Prefer the great outdoors to indoor museums? Woodsy trails lace **Rock Creek Park** *(tel 202-895-6000, nps.gov/rocr)*, once a favorite bird-watching destination for President Theodore Roosevelt. The **United States National Arboretum** *(3501 New York Ave., N.E., tel 202-245-2726, usna.usda.gov)* is a great place to stroll (though you'll need a car to get there). And **Theodore Roosevelt Island** *(tel 703-289-2500, nps.gov/this)*, just north of Rosslyn, VA, is a hidden escape in the heart of the city.

❼ Arena Stage *(arenastage.org)*.
Enjoy American plays at this renowned theater. As of writing, the surrounding Southwest Waterfront neighborhood, beloved for its popular ■ FISH MARKET, is undergoing exciting renovation. Keep an eye out for intriguing new bars and eateries ideal for pre- or après-theater imbibing.

Fresh Maryland crabs at the S.W. Fish Market

D.C. for Fun

D.C. isn't all about politics—enjoy a day in the places where Washingtonians frolic.

❶ Georgetown Shopping (see p. 28) Begin your day with a leisurely brunch followed by a dose of retail therapy at some of the city's trendiest shops. From M St., N.W., walk down to the Potomac River and turn left along the riverfront walkway.

❷ Lunch at Washington Harbour (see p. 28) Savor lunch on a shady outdoor terrace overlooking the Potomac River. Continue along the riverfront southeast to Thompson Boat Center.

❸ Kayak or Bike on the Potomac (see pp. 28–29) Enjoy some of D.C.'s prettiest scenery from the water or along a tree-shaded trail. Take the Metro's orange, blue, or silver line from the Foggy Bottom station to the Metro Center station and walk three blocks east on G St., N.W., then south two blocks on 15th St., N.W., to the W Washington D.C. hotel.

**D.C. FOR FUN   DISTANCE: 2.5 MILES (4 KM)
TIME: APPROX. 13 HOURS   METRO: FOGGY BOTTOM**

7 **Nightcap at the Hamilton**
(see p. 29) End your fun day
with a nightcap at the Hamilton's
tucked-away piano bar.

6 **The Capitol Steps** (see p. 29)
Enjoy some hilarious political satire
then walk north two blocks along
14th St., N.W.

5 **Drinks & Dinner on
14th Street** (see pp. 132–
133) Kick up your heels on
one of D.C.'s hippest streets.
From the U St.–African-
American Civil War
Memorial–Cardozo station,
take the yellow or green line
to the Archives–Navy
Memorial–Penn Quarter
station and walk five blocks
west on Pennsylvania Ave.

4 **Bliss Out at the W** (see p. 29) Pamper
yourself head to toe—complete with gratis
brownie bites—at the spa at the W Washington
D.C. hotel. Then walk seven blocks east to the
Gallery Place–Chinatown Metro station and take
the green or yellow line to the U St.–African-
American Civil War Memorial–Cardozo station;
from here, walk two blocks west on U St., N.W.

Georgetown Shopping

1 Begin with brunch at **Peacock Café** (*3251 Prospect St., N.W., tel 202-625-2740*), beloved for its eggs Benedict, French toast, and omelets. Then poke into shops along the picturesque brick sidewalks of M Street and Wisconsin Avenue, N.W., including **The Shops at Georgetown Park** (*3222 M St., N.W., tel 202-342-8190*).

Lunch at Washington Harbour

2 Restaurants spangle this popular riverfront area, ideal for strolling and, with plenty of benches, for people-watching too. **Sequoia** (*3000 K St., N.W., tel 202-944-4200*) is a bustling lunch venue, featuring American entrées, sandwiches, and salads—on a sunny day, ask for a table on the shady terrace overlooking the river.

Kayak or Bike on the Potomac

3 The nearby **Thompson Boat Center** (*2900 Virginia Ave., N.W., tel 202-333-9543, thompsonboatcenter.com*) offers

M Street favorite Georgetown Cupcake has found nationwide fame on television.

hour-long kayak rentals—hop aboard and begin paddling around **Theodore Roosevelt Island,** or beneath nearby **Key Bridge,** for a different take on the Capital City. If you prefer cycling, rent two wheels from **Capital Bikeshare** (*capitalbikeshare.com*)—there's a depot near Waters Alley—and take a spin on the paths edging both sides of the Potomac while enjoying sublime views of the monuments.

Bliss Out at the W

4 Late afternoon is the perfect time to pamper yourself, and the mod W Washington D.C. hotel's Bliss day spa is the ideal place to indulge. Whether you opt for the ginger rub massage or triple oxygen treatment, complimentary brownie bites are obligatory.

515 15th St., N.W. • tel 202-661-2416 • blissworld.com • Metro: Metro Center

Drinks & Dinner on 14th Street

5 See pp. 132–133.

The Capitol Steps

6 Sit back for some political-inspired laughs with this hilarious musical extravaganza focusing on the topics of the day.

Ronald Reagan Building, 1300 Pennsylvania Ave., N.W. • tel 202-312-1555 • capsteps.com • Fri.–Sat. only • $$$$$ • Metro: Metro Center

Nightcap at the Hamilton

7 Relaxing at the British-style pub tucked away on the second floor of this cavernous bar/eatery is the perfect way to end a day of fun.

600 14th St., N.W. • tel 202-787-1000 • thehamiltondc.com • Metro: Metro Center

---

IN **THE KNOW**

Washington, D.C., was devastated by riots after Martin Luther King's assassination in 1968. But beginning with **Penn Quarter** in the late 1990s and **U Street** and **14th Street** after that, one neighborhood after the next is being revitalized. Northeast's **H Street** is fast becoming the place to enjoy a night out. **The Yards,** east of Nationals Park, is also thriving. Now it's the **Southwest Waterfront's** turn, with a huge redevelopment plan bringing restaurants, a movie theater, clubs, bars, and a concert hall along the Washington Channel.

WHIRLWIND TOURS

D.C. With Kids

Zoo animals, monsters, and spies are just some of Washington's offerings for kids.

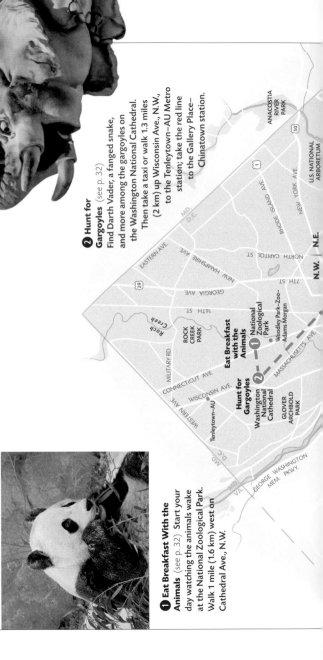

❶ Eat Breakfast With the Animals (see p. 32) Start your day watching the animals wake at the National Zoological Park. Walk 1 mile (1.6 km) west on Cathedral Ave., N.W.

❷ Hunt for Gargoyles (see p. 32) Find Darth Vader, a fanged snake, and more among the gargoyles on the Washington National Cathedral. Then take a taxi or walk 1.3 miles (2 km) up Wisconsin Ave., N.W., to the Tenleytown–AU Metro station; take the red line to the Gallery Place–Chinatown station.

3 Spy Around (see pp. 32, 94–95) Visit the International Spy Museum—and/or embark on a neighborhood spy tour. Next walk south on 7th St, N.W., to Constitution Ave, N.W., turn right to 15th St, N.W., then left to the Tidal Basin

5 Whirl Above National Harbor (see p. 33) Finish up your day at this bustling center of shops, restaurants—and Ferris wheel, just across the line in Maryland.

4 Go Paddleboating (see p. 33) Tootle around the Tidal Basin for a waterborne view of the Jefferson Memorial and the famous cherry trees—beautiful even when they're not in bloom. Take the Potomac River Company water taxi from Ohio Dr, S.W., to National Harbor.

D.C. WITH KIDS   DISTANCE: 4 MILES (6.4 KM)   TIME: APPROX. 8 HOURS
METRO: WOODLEY PARK–ZOO–ADAMS MORGAN

D.C. **WITH KIDS**

WHIRLWIND TOURS

Eat Breakfast With the Animals

1 Explore the National Zoological Park early in the morning before the crowds descend—and when the animals are starting their day. The gates open at 6 a.m., prime time to watch the red pandas, lionesses, and gibbons play, cavort, and run about. (Note that you'll have to wait for their building to open to see the famous giant pandas.)

3001 Connecticut Ave., N.W. • tel 202-633-4888 • nationalzoo.si.edu • Metro: Woodley Park–Zoo–Adams Morgan

Hunt for Gargoyles

2 The Gothic-style Washington National Cathedral ranks as the world's sixth largest cathedral, utilizing 30 million pounds of Indiana limestone and the talent of five architects and thousands of masons, sculptors, and other workers over 83 years (finishing in 1990). Kids love the "Gargoyle Tour," focusing on the fantastical and imaginary creatures and people serving as rain spouts on its exterior.

3101 Wisconsin Ave., N.W. • tel 202-537-6200 • cathedral.org • Gargoyle Tour: April–October only • $$ • Metro: Tenleytown–AU, then Bus: 31, 32, 36, or 37 south (or walk 1.5 miles/2.4 km down Wisconsin Ave.)

IN **THE KNOW**

Museums throughout D.C. have special sections and fun activities just for kids, such as the **National Building Museum** (see p. 95), with hands-on building activities. At the **National Museum of Natural History** (see p. 56) an interactive learning experience called Q?rius helps kids understand science as it relates to nature and their lives. The Smithsonian's Ripley Center's **Discovery Theater** (*1100 Jefferson Dr., S.W., tel 202-633-8700, discoverytheater.org*) focuses on art, science, and heritage.

Spy Around

3 (See pp. 94–95) After getting their own secret identity, kids (and adults) set out to test their skills at the interactive International Spy Museum. You'll slide through an air-conditioning duct to spy on people below; test your observation, analysis, and disguise skills; and learn the stories behind the spycraft. Gadgets galore (mostly from the '50s and '60s) add to the allure. A special "Spies in the City Experience" involves a mission assignment and hunting for clues around Washington.

800 F St., N.W. • tel 202-393-7798 • spymuseum.org • $$$$ adults, $$$ kids • Metro: Gallery Place–Chinatown

Paddleboating on the Tidal Basin is a cool way to beat the Washington heat.

Go Paddleboating

4 Let the kids work off their extra energy while viewing the Jefferson Memorial, Martin Luther King, Jr. Memorial, and the cherry trees from a waterborne perspective on the Tidal Basin.

1501 Maine Ave., S.W. • tel 202-479-2426 • tidalbasinpaddleboats.com • Kids need to have an adult onboard • Mid-May–Columbus Day • $$$ • Metro: Smithsonian

Whirl Above National Harbor

5 Take a Potomac River water taxi from Ohio Drive *(tel 703-684-0580 or 877-511-2628, potomacriverboatco.com)* to **National Harbor,** a thriving waterfront commercial center with restaurants, shops, and Gaylord National Resort. Overshadowing it all is the giant **Capital Wheel** *(116 Waterfront St., National Harbor, MD, tel 301-842-8650, thecapitalwheel.com)*—a big Ferris wheel that sweeps you 180 feet (55 m) into the air for magnificent views in all directions. Kids can point out the White House, U.S. Capitol, and, far off in the distance, Arlington National Cemetery. A nearby carousel offers rides on whimsical and wild animals.

WHIRLWIND TOURS

African-American Heritage

Discover the legacies of some of the greatest—and lesser known—African Americans in Washington and beyond.

1 Martin Luther King, Jr. Memorial (see pp. 36, 54) Pay homage to the leader of the civil rights movement at his memorial on the Tidal Basin. Walk east on Independence Ave., S.W., and north on 15th St., S.W./N.W.

2 National Museum of African American History and Culture (see p. 36) Devote as much time as you can to this new museum celebrating the African-American legacy in the U.S. From the Archives–Navy Memorial–Penn Quarter Metro station, take the green line to the Anacostia station and walk 0.75 mile (1.2 km). Go right on Howard Rd., S.E., left on Martin Luther King, Jr. Ave., S.E., and right on W St., S.E.

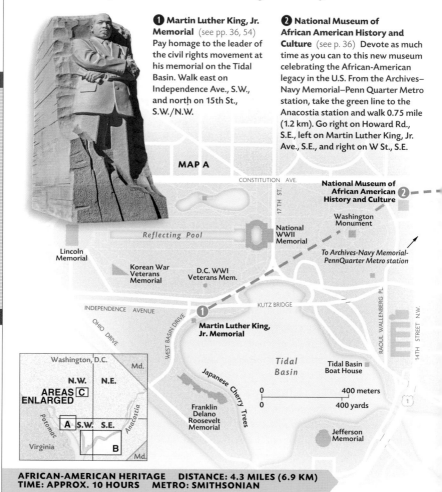

MAP A

CONSTITUTION AVE.

17TH ST.

National Museum of African American History and Culture **2**

Washington Monument

National WWII Memorial

Reflecting Pool

To Archives-Navy Memorial-PennQuarter Metro station

Lincoln Memorial

Korean War Veterans Memorial

D.C. WWI Veterans Mem.

INDEPENDENCE AVENUE

KUTZ BRIDGE

RAOUL WALLENBERG PL.

14TH STREET N.W.

OHIO DRIVE

WEST BASIN DRIVE

1 Martin Luther King, Jr. Memorial

Tidal Basin

Tidal Basin Boat House

Washington, D.C.

Md.

N.W. **N.E.**

AREAS C ENLARGED

Potomac

A S.W. **S.E.**

Virginia **B**

Md.

Anacostia

Japanese Cherry Trees

Franklin Delano Roosevelt Memorial

0 ___ 400 meters
0 ___ 400 yards

Jefferson Memorial

1

AFRICAN-AMERICAN HERITAGE   DISTANCE: 4.3 MILES (6.9 KM)
TIME: APPROX. 10 HOURS   METRO: SMITHSONIAN

Lincoln Theatre 6 Ben's Chili Bowl V ST.

U ST. N.W.

U Street–African-Amer
Civil War Museum–Cardozo

**African American
Civil War Memorial
and Museum** 5

FLORIDA AVE

VERMONT AVE

14TH ST.   13TH ST.   11TH ST.   9TH ST.   7TH ST.

S ST.

Shaw-
Howard

R ST.

RHODE ISLAND AVE

Q ST.

P ST.   Logan
Circle

0   0.25 kilometers

0   0.25 miles

MAP C

6 **Lincoln Theatre** (see p. 37)
Round out your day with a show at the
famed 1920s theater and music club.

5 **African American Civil War Memorial and
Museum** (see p. 37) Visit another Smithsonian-affiliated
museum, this one focusing on the African-American role
in the Civil War. Walk two blocks east on U St., N.W.

MAP B

3 **Frederick Douglass
National Historic Site** (see p. 36)
Visit the last home of the sage of
Anacostia. Walk 1 mile (1.6 km)
west via Morris Rd., S.E.

Navy Yard–
Ballpark

M ST. N.E.

SOUTHEAST BLVD.

Anacostia

ANACOSTIA PARK

Washington
Navy Yard

OFFICER KEVIN J. WELSH
MEMORIAL BRIDGE

Washington Channel

Nationals
Park

S CAPITOL ST. S.W.

295

NAYLOR RD.

MINN. AVE.   22ND ST.

16TH ST. S.E.

S ST. S.E.

S.W. | S.E.

GOOD HOPE ROAD S.E.

4 **Anacostia Community
Museum** (see p. 37) This
Smithsonian-affiliated museum
has fascinating exhibits related to
the African-American experience
in D.C. Backtrack 1.2 miles (1.9 km)
via Morris Rd., S.E., to the Anacostia
Metro station and take the green line
to the U St.–African-American Civil
War Memorial–Cardozo station.

HOWARD
ROAD

Anacostia

MARTIN   LUTHER KING JR. AVE   W STREET

MORRIS RD.

SHERIDAN RD.

STANTON RD.

HUNTER PLACE

**Frederick
Douglass
National
Historic Site** 3

**FORT
STANTON
PARK**

BRUCE PL.

**Anacostia
Community
Museum** 4

0   400 meters

0   400 yards

Martin Luther King, Jr. Memorial

1 (See p. 54) This granite monument honors Dr. King's dedication and perseverance in fighting for civil rights. Take time to read some of his most famous, and discerning, quotes. Then walk over to the **Lincoln Memorial,** where a plaque marks the step where King stood to give his famous "I Have a Dream" speech in 1963.

1964 Independence Ave., S.W. • tel 202-426-6841 • nps.gov/mlkm
• Metro: Smithsonian

National Museum of African American History and Culture

2 This new Smithsonian museum celebrates African-American heritage in the nation's capital from the Civil War and beyond. Don't miss the **"Black Fashion Collection,"** the **"Ernest C. Withers Photography Collection,"** and the **"Harriet Tubman Collection."**

1400 Constitution Ave., N.W. • tel 202-633-1000 • nmaahc.si.edu
• Metro: Smithsonian

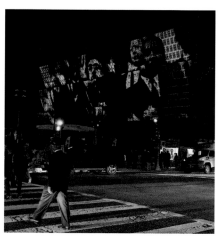

The building itself is a canvas at the new National Museum of African American History and Culture.

Frederick Douglass National Historic Site

3 Born a slave, Frederick Douglass bought his freedom and became an important contributor to the civil rights movement. His grand hilltop house contains more than 70 percent of the Douglass family belongings, including the leader's favorite chair, his eyeglasses, and his walking stick. The house can only be seen by a guided tour—reserve ahead online.

1411 W St., S.E. • tel 202-426-5961
• nps.gov/frdo • By guided tour only
• $ (admin. fee) • Metro: Anacostia

Anacostia Community Museum

4 Extremely well-curated temporary exhibits examine the history and culture of the Anacostia neighborhood and beyond, oftentimes featuring the works of local artists and thought leaders. Examples in the past have included "How the Civil War Changed Washington," "Separate and Unequaled: Black Baseball in the District of Columbia," and "Twelve Years that Shook and Shaped Washington: 1963–1975."

1901 Fort Place, S.E. • tel 202-633-4820 • anacostia.si.edu • Metro: Anacostia

African American Civil War Memorial and Museum

5 Newspaper articles, uniforms, weapons, and more honor African-American contributions to the Civil War in this museum. "Better even to die free than to live slaves," uttered Frederick Douglass—his words captured in bronze upon a **sculpture** across the street, honoring the African-American troops who fought in the Union Army.

Memorial: U St. & Vermont Ave., N.W. • Museum: 1925 Vermont Ave., N.W. • tel 202-667-2667 • Museum: closed Sun.–Mon. • afroamcivilwar.org • Metro: U St.–African-American Civil War Memorial–Cardozo

Lincoln Theatre

6 End your walking tour with a theater, dance, or comedy show at this legendary movie palace and live-performance venue, dating from 1922. Back in the day, luminaries taking to the stage ranged from Washington natives Duke Ellington and Pearl Bailey to Cab Calloway, Ella Fitzgerald, and Sarah Vaughan.

1215 U St., N.W. • tel 202-888-0050 or 877-435-9849 • thelincolndc.com; check website for performances • Metro: U St.–African-American Civil War Memorial–Cardozo

WHIRLWIND TOURS

Embassy Row

Peek into the diplomatic side of the Capital City along Massachusetts Avenue, N.W. –aka Embassy Row, where many of the world's diplomatic missions are clustered– and see how many national flags you can identify flying out in front.

8 Washington National Cathedral (see p. 41) Absorb the immensity of the National Cathedral then rest your weary feet at its Open City café.

7 Observatory Circle (see p. 41) The vice president of the United States–and the Naval Observatory–reside behind this circle's high iron fence. Continue up Massachusetts, turning right onto Wisconsin Ave., N.W.

6 Embassy of South Africa (see p. 41) A statue of Nelson Mandela means your long walk has brought you to the South Africa embassy. Continue up Massachusetts Ave, N.W.

MACOMB STREET

CATHEDRAL AVE.

CONNECTICUT

27TH ST.

29TH ST.

WOODLEY RD.

CALVERT ST.

24TH ST.

Woodley Park–Zoo/
Adams Morgan

Omni
Shoreham

DUKE
ELLINGTON
MEMORIAL
BRIDGE

AVENUE

CLEVELAND AVENUE

32ND ST.

30TH ST.

**Observatory
Circle**

7

**U.S. Naval
Observatory**

34TH ST.

GARFIELD ST.

WOODLEY RD.

**Washington
National
Cathedral**

8

36TH ST.

WISCONSIN AVE.

MASSACHUSETTS AVE.

EDMUNDS ST.

CALVERT ST.

5 Embassy of Brazil (see p. 41) This modern embassy resembles a tinted glass cube on stilts. Continue up Massachusetts Ave., N.W.

4 Islamic Center of Washington (see p. 40) One of the oldest mosques in the U.S., where more than 6,000 pray on Fridays. Cross the Massachusetts Avenue Bridge, and continue northwest.

1 Dupont Circle (see pp. 40, 130–131) Begin your walk at this fountain-graced circle, hub of the neighborhood. Then head up Massachusetts Ave., N.W.

2 Embassy of Indonesia (see p. 40) You can't miss the statue of Saraswati in front of this embassy near Dupont Circle. Cross Massachusetts Ave., and continue up its eastern side about 0.25 mile (0.4 km).

3 Sheridan Circle (see p. 40) Several embassies cluster around this circle with its statue of the Union general. Continue up Massachusetts Ave., staying on the street's eastern side.

0 — 200 meters
0 — 200 yards

EMBASSY ROW   DISTANCE: 2.3 MILES (3.7 KM)
TIME: APPROX. 2 HOURS   METRO: DUPONT CIRCLE

Dupont Circle

1 (See pp. 130–131) Begin the walk up Massachusetts Avenue—aka Embassy Row—at this graceful fountain featuring allegorical figures representing the sea, wind, and stars, and Civil War naval hero Samuel Francis du Pont.

Intersection of Connecticut Ave., Massachusetts Ave., P St., 19th St., & New Hampshire Ave., N.W. • Metro: Dupont Circle

Embassy of Indonesia

2 Evalyn Walsh McLean, the last private owner of the Hope Diamond, lived in this lavish 1903 mansion built by her father on profits made in Colorado gold mining. She sold it to the Republic of Indonesia in 1951.

2020 Massachusetts Ave., N.W. • private • Metro: Dupont Circle

Sheridan Circle

3 Ringed by the **embassies of Pakistan, Cyprus, Armenia,** and **Romania,** this circle hosts a statue of Union Civil War general Philip Sheridan sculpted by Gutzon Borglum.

Massachusetts Ave., N.W., at 23rd St., N.W. • Metro: Dupont Circle

Islamic Center of Washington

4 A 162-foot (49 m) minaret rises above what was once the Western Hemisphere's largest mosque. Visitors are free to enter; women must wear a scarf, and shoes must be removed.

2551 Massachusetts Ave., N.W. • tel 202-332-8343 • theislamiccenter.com • Metro: Dupont Circle

A statue of the Hindu goddess Saraswati rises outside the Embassy of Indonesia.

Embassy of Brazil

5 All glass and angles, the modernist Brazilian Embassy was designed by Brazilian architect Olavo Redig de Campos in the 1970s.

3006 Massachusetts Ave., N.W. • tel 202-238-2700 • private • Metro: Dupont Circle, Woodley Park–Zoo–Adams Morgan

Embassy of South Africa

6 You can't miss the South African embassy, with its large statue of Nelson Mandela, where sit-ins and protests took place to free him from prison and to end apartheid. Across the street a statue of Winston Churchill flashes his signature "V-for-victory" sign at the **British Embassy.**

3051 Massachusetts Ave., N.W. • tel 202-232-4400 • private • Metro: Dupont Circle, Woodley Park–Zoo–Adams Morgan

Observatory Circle

7 A ship anchor and the digital USNO Master Clock mark tree-shaded Observatory Circle, home to the **U.S. Naval Observatory** and the residence of the vice president of the United States. Among the embassies clustered around the circle, the modern **Embassy of Finland** (*3301 Massachusetts Ave., N.W., tel 202-298-5800*) has a cantilevered glass back wall projected over Rock Creek Park. It's open occasionally for exhibitions, as well as special concerts.

Massachusetts Ave., N.W., bet. 30th & 34th Sts., N.W. • Metro: Dupont Circle, Woodley Park–Zoo–Adams Morgan

Washington National Cathedral

8 End your walk with some contemplative time at the world's sixth largest cathedral. Then rest your feet and enjoy a cup of coffee at the **Open City at the National Cathedral** café in the Old Baptistry.

3101 Wisconsin Ave., N.W. • tel 202-537-6200 • cathedral.org • $$ to visit cathedral Mon.–Sat., worshippers enter for free • Metro: Woodley Park–Zoo–Adams Morgan

Downtown Georgetown's M Street

PART 2

Washington's Neighborhoods

Washington's Neighborhoods

MONTROSE PARK

Rock Creek

SHERIDAN CIRCLE

Dupont Circle

DUPONT CIRCLE

P ST.

CONNECTICUT AVE.

COLUMBIA ROAD

ADAMS MORGAN

U STREET

18TH

MASSACHUSETTS AVE.

NEW HAMPSHIRE

RHODE

M ST.

GEORGETOWN

Georgetown University

CHESAPEAKE AND OHIO CANAL NATIONAL HISTORICAL PARK

Chesapeake & Ohio Canal

M STREET NW

WHITEHURST FREEWAY

KEY BRIDGE

Potomac

ROCK CREEK AND POTOMAC PKWY

K STREET.

FARRAGUT NORTH

Farragut West

LAFAYETTE SQUARE

FOGGY BOTTOM

H ST.

PENNSYLVANIA AVE.

23RD STREET

22ND STREET

25TH ST.

21ST ST.

I ST.

F ST.

E STREET

18TH

17TH STREET

19TH

Roosevelt Island

Virginia

Kennedy Center

66

AVENUE

C STREET

CONSTITUTION AVE.

THEODORE ROOSEVELT MEMORIAL BRIDGE

NORTHWEST

SOUTHWEST

Lincoln Memorial

National WWII Memorial

Reflecting Pool

WEST POTOMAC PARK

ARLINGTON MEMORIAL BRIDGE

INDEPENDENCE AVE.

OHIO

Tidal Basin

Market Square

WATERFRONT PARK

Potomac

Jefferson Memorial

PENDLETON STREET

PRINCESS

FAYETTE

KING

PITT ST.

WASHINGTON ST.

ST. ASAPH

PRINCE

DUKE

UNION ST.

GIBBON ST.

0   200 meters

0   200 yards

National Mall

Graced with world-class museums, marble monuments, and green spaces made for strolling, picnicking, and tossing a Frisbee, the nation's playground is a 2-mile-long (3 km), tree-shaded expanse first envisioned by architect Pierre-Charles L'Enfant in 1791. His original grandiose vision included stately residences along a "vast esplanade," a plan revised by the end of the 1800s for financial reasons. No worries—the National Mall, anchored by the Capitol at one end and the Lincoln Memorial at the other—does not disappoint. Indeed, here is where you'll find the celebrated Smithsonian museums (all free of charge), including the ever popular National Air and Space Museum and the National Museum of American History. Here, too, between 14th Street, N.W., and the Potomac River, are a string of majestic monuments to national heroes such as George Washington, Abraham Lincoln, and Thomas Jefferson, set alongside memorials to times of sacrifice such as World War II. You could spend a week—if not a month—exploring and still not see everything. Pace yourself!

◀ **The Mall is the capital's premier public park, peppered with monuments and museums.**

National Mall

Plan a full day to explore the country's most significant collection of museum
and monuments on the National Mall–dubbed America's Front Yard.

❸ **Vietnam Veterans Memorial**
(see pp. 51–52) **Shocking when first
unveiled in 1982, this minimalistic,
black-granite memorial has become
one of the nation's most revered.
Go southwest, to the end of the
Reflecting Pool.**

❷ **National World War II
Memorial** (see p. 51) **A graceful,
waterfall-centered memorial to
the heroes of the "Greatest
Generation." Continue west
through the Constitution Gardens
just north of the Reflecting Pool.**

❶ **Washington
Monument** (see p. 50)
**The nation's 555-foot
(169 m) marble tribute
to the first president.
Walk west, crossing
17th St., N.W.**

❹ **Lincoln Memorial**
(see pp. 52–53) **The
imposing statue of a
seated Lincoln deep
in contemplation
draws some six
million visitors
each year. Follow
the pathway just
to the southeast.**

NATIONAL MALL

**Vietnam
Veterans
Memorial**
❸

CONSTITUTION GARDENS
Reflecting Pool

**Lincoln
Memorial** ❹

❺

**Korean War
Veterans
Memorial**

WEST POTOMAC PARK

**D.C. War
Memorial**

CONSTITUTION ⑤⓪ AVENUE

STREET

❷

17TH

**Washington
Monument** ❶

**National
WWII
Memorial**

**Sylvan
Theater**

RAOUL WALLENBERG PL.

INDEPENDENCE AVENUE

❻ **Martin
Luther
King, Jr.
Memorial**

WEST BASIN DRIVE

Potomac

OHIO DRIVE

❼ **Franklin Delano
Roosevelt Memorial**

0 ——— 400 meters
0 ——— 400 yards

*Tidal
Basin*

**Tidal
Basin
Boathouse**

❽ **Thomas
Jefferson
Memorial**

❺ **Korean War Veterans
Memorial** (see pp. 53) **One of the
Mall's more hidden memorials, yet every
bit as potent as the others in its declaration
that freedom is not free. Walk southeast
toward the Tidal Basin, crossing Independence
Ave., S.W., at the second traffic light.**

**NATIONAL MALL   DISTANCE: 4.1 MILES (6.6 KM)
TIME: 8 HOURS   METRO START: SMITHSONIAN**

⑫ National Air and Space Museum (see pp. 60–63) One of the planet's most visited museums, celebrating the air and space revolutions through the ages.

⑪ National Gallery of Art (see pp. 56–57) Experience this remarkable collection of world-famous masters in two parts—the classical West Building and the modern East Building. Then head across the National Mall.

⑩ National Museum of Natural History (see p. 56) Marvel at the mammoth elephant, the Hope Diamond, a real-life coral reef, and more. Then walk east.

⑨ National Museum of American History (see pp. 58–59) A tribute to American history and culture: Julia Child's kitchen, the first ladies' gowns, the Star-Spangled Banner—they're all here. Continue east on the National Mall to the next big building between 12th and 9th Sts., N.W.

⑥ Martin Luther King, Jr. Memorial (see p. 54) The 30-foot (9 m) likeness of the civil rights leader symbolically emerges from the Stone of Hope. Follow the pathway south of the memorial, along the Tidal Basin.

⑦ Franklin Delano Roosevelt Memorial (see pp. 54–55) Four separate outdoor granite alcoves represent the 32nd president's four terms in office. Continue to the Tidal Basin's south side.

⑧ Thomas Jefferson Memorial (see p. 55) This neoclassical temple celebrates the innovative third president. Continue around the Tidal Basin to Raoul Wallenberg Place, S.W., which becomes 15th St., N.W.; turn right at Madison Dr.

NATIONAL MALL

Washington Monument

1 Soaring above D.C.'s low skyline and surrounded by American flags representing every state, this 555-foot-5.9-inch (169 m) spire honors America's first president. Begun in 1848, the iconic marble-and-granite obelisk sat half finished between 1854 and 1879 due to a design disagreement, lack of funding, and the Civil War. At long last the monument was dedicated in 1885; the change of stone color about 150 feet (46 m) above the base marks where work resumed with stone from a different quarry. While no longer the world's tallest man-made structure, it remains the world's tallest obelisk. To go up, free, timed tickets are available at the monument's base (or reserve them online at *recreation.gov*). A 60-second elevator ride ascends to vast views over the city. On the descent the elevator slows down, allowing you to see the change in old and new marble from the inside, as well as commemorative stones and inscriptions.

2 15th St., N.W. • tel 202-426-6841 • nps.gov/wamo • tickets: tel 877-444-6777 or recreation.gov • Metro: Smithsonian

Descending walls of the Vietnam Veterans Memorial reflect the memories of those who served.

National World War II Memorial

2 A graceful, fountain-spouting pool encircled by columns and arches comprises this sober memorial to the 16.1 million soldiers who served the nation during World War II—and honors those who gave the ultimate sacrifice. Look closer, and you'll begin to understand the symbolism. The **Freedom Wall** with 4,048 gold stars pays tribute to the more than 400,000 Americans killed during the conflict (each star represents 100 American military deaths). Arcing out from there, 56 granite pillars stand for each U.S. state and federal territory (and the District of Columbia) involved in the war. They're arranged based on each one's entry date into the Union, starting with Delaware to the right of the Freedom Wall, followed by Pennsylvania to the left, with the order alternating north to south. The 43-foot-high (13 m) arches anchoring the columns symbolize the war's Atlantic and Pacific theaters. In addition, two dozen bronze panels depict scenes from the war. Every war veteran will recognize the two "Kilroy Was Here" drawings hidden in the memorial. These mimic the popular cartoon image of a man looking over a wall, graffiti often left by servicemen to indicate they had passed through an area. If you have time, search the computerized registry for a family member or friend you know who served in the war—both overseas and on the home front.

17th St. & Independence Ave., N.W. • tel 202-426-6841 or 800-639-4WW2 • nps.gov/wwii • Metro: Smithsonian

SAVVY **TRAVELER**

The Smithsonian Institution, established in 1846, comprises a total of 19 museums, 9 research centers, and the National Zoo—with 11 museums on the Mall. Visit the website for an overview, or stop by **The Castle,** which offers a visitor center and planning map, as well as mini displays on each museum to help you decide where to go. *1000 Jefferson Dr., S.W., tel 202-633-1000, si.edu*

Vietnam Veterans Memorial

3 Designed by Maya Lin and dedicated in 1982, the distinctive Vietnam Veterans Memorial is a startling modern contrast to the ode to classicism of the monuments surrounding it. Two 246-foot-long (75 m) walls create a black-granite wedge cutting into the earth, symbolically representing a wound that has closed and is

IN **THE KNOW**

When we use the term "National Mall," we typically mean the entire 2-mile-long (3 km) monument- and museum-dotted swath of parkland between the Lincoln Memorial in the west and the U.S. Capitol building in the east. In reality, this is wrong. The official National Mall occupies the land between the grounds of the U.S. Capitol and the Washington Monument. So what lies west of that? The land holding all of the monuments and memorials between the Washington Monument and the Lincoln Memorial is officially called West Potomac Park.

healing. The names of 58,307 Americans are etched into the glistening wall—a diamond marks those who died in action, while a cross indicates those missing in action. As you walk along the memorial, the wall becomes taller as the number of names increases, reaching a high point of 10.1 feet (3 m). You'll also notice how the granite's sheen reflects the images of visitors—including yourself—seemingly projecting life as much as honoring death. Piles of mementos from loved ones are left daily—medals, teddy bears, and at least one motorcycle; items are collected by the National Park Service and cataloged and stored. Nearby, a bronze statue titled "The Three Servicemen" puts faces to the names. Another bronze group called the "Vietnam Women's Memorial," added in 1993, honors the women who participated in the war. If you're looking for a specific name, use the Directory of Names, located at both ends of the wall and arranged alphabetically.

North side of Lincoln Memorial, near intersection of 22nd St. & Constitution Ave., N.W. • tel 202-426-6841 • nps.gov/vive • Metro: Foggy Bottom–GWU

Lincoln Memorial

4 Looking every bit like a classic Greek temple, the magnificent Lincoln Memorial, designed by Henry Bacon, honors the 16th president of the United States. The 36 fluted Doric columns represent the number of states in the Union at the time of Lincoln's death. Inside, at the top of the steps, you are greeted by the 19-foot-high (6 m) statue of a seated Lincoln, carved under the direction of Daniel Chester French in white Georgia marble. Lincoln's clenched left hand shows strength and resolve; his right hand lies open to signal compassion (it's an urban myth that he is signing "A.L."). Inspiring words from the Gettysburg Address and Lincoln's second

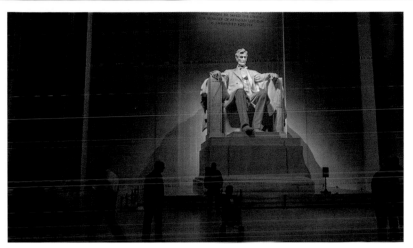

The gravitas of Abraham Lincoln's leadership is felt at his memorial, especially at night.

inaugural address are inscribed on the memorial's side chambers. Don't miss the display of Lincoln's writings and speeches on the lower level, where you can also watch a video on the site's long history of protests and demonstrations. Martin Luther King, Jr., delivered his famous "I Have a Dream" speech in front of the memorial in 1963; an engraved plaque marks the stair where he stood.

2 Lincoln Memorial Circle, N.W. • tel 202-426-6841 • nps.gov/linc • Metro: Foggy Bottom–GWU

Korean War Veterans Memorial

5 Nineteen larger-than-life, stainless-steel soldiers walk in formation through juniper bushes, a sea of photographic faces watching them from a granite wall. Dedicated in 1992, this moving memorial commemorates the 5.8 million Americans who served in the three-year conflict. Inscriptions on the **Pool of Remembrance** note the number of soldiers killed, wounded, MIA, and imprisoned as POWs.

900 Ohio Dr., S.W. • tel 202-426-6841 • nps.gov/kowa • Metro: Foggy Bottom–GWU

Martin Luther King, Jr. Memorial

6 Dedicated in 2011, this eye-catching memorial on the edge of the Tidal Basin honors the clergyman, activist, and nonviolence advocate who so diligently and poignantly advanced the civil rights movement both in the United States and around the world. Referencing his landmark "I Have a Dream" speech, King's 19-foot (6 m) likeness emerges from the rough-hewn Stone of Hope, beyond a boulder split in two representing the Mountain of Despair. After pondering the symbolism of your own figurative walk through the Mountain of Despair, take time to read some of King's most famous, and discerning, quotes etched into the adjacent 450-foot-long (137 m) inscription wall; the earliest dates from the 1955 Montgomery bus boycott in Alabama, the latest from King's last sermon, delivered in 1968 just a day before his assassination in Memphis.

1964 Independence Ave., S.W. • tel 202-426-6841 • nps.gov/mlkm
• Metro: Smithsonian

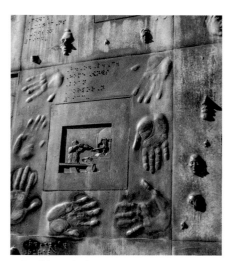

A detail from the five massive bronze canvases expressing the impact of FDR's social programs

Franklin Delano Roosevelt Memorial

7 Set on the Tidal Basin's west side, this striking, 7.5-acre (3 ha) memorial, opened in 1997, honors the 32nd president of the United States. It is also the only presidential memorial to include a first lady, as well as a first pet. Four unroofed, red-granite-walled alcoves—one for each of his four terms, between 1933 and 1945—spread along the water's edge. These mark Roosevelt's greatest struggles and triumphs, including the Depression, the New Deal, and World

War II. Stroll through the rooms, admiring the landscaped plazas, waterfalls, quiet pools, and statues, and reading the famous FDR quotations engraved on the walls, among them the inspiring words from his first inaugural address, "The only thing we have to fear is fear itself."

400 W. Basin Dr., S.W. • tel 202-426-6841 • nps.gov/frde
• Metro: Smithsonian

Thomas Jefferson Memorial

8 Dedicated to the drafter of the Declaration of Independence and the third U.S. president, this graceful white-marble structure was designed by John Russell Pope in the style of the ancient Roman Pantheon and completed in 1943. Inside the colonnade building, a 19-foot (6 m) bronze statue of a stately Thomas Jefferson stands beneath a towering dome. Among the quotes on the wall is one from a letter written in 1800: "for I have sworn upon the altar of god eternal hostility against every form of tyranny over the mind of man." A lower lobby has exhibits, a gift shop, and a bookstore. From the front, you can't miss the iconic view of the Tidal Basin, with its twirling gulls and paddleboats and springtime cherry blossoms, the Washington Monument rising behind. Beyond that, in a deliberately straight line, rises the White House and all the symbolism of democracy that emanates from it.

13 E. Basin Dr., S.W. • tel 202-426-6841 • nps.gov/thje
• Metro: Smithsonian

National Museum of American History

9 See pp. 58–59.

National Mall between 12th & 14th Sts., N.W. • tel 202-633-1000
• americanhistory.si.edu • Metro: Smithsonian, Federal Triangle

GOOD **EATS**

■ **GARDEN CAFÉ**
Artsy menus are coordinated with themed exhibits at the hosting National Gallery of Art in this West Building Café. **National Mall bet. 4th & 7th Sts., N.W., tel 202-712-7454, $**

■ **MITSITAM CAFÉ**
Authentic indigenous cuisine of the Americas served cafeteria style within the National Museum of the American Indian. **950 Independence Ave., S.W., tel 202-633-1000, $**

■ **PAVILION CAFÉ**
Sandwiches, soup, and salads with flair within the National Gallery of Art's lovely sculpture garden. **Bet. Madison Dr. & Constitution Ave., N.W., tel 202-289-3361, $**

NATIONAL MALL

National Museum of Natural History

10 Entering the Rotunda from the Mall side of this enormous museum, you're greeted by an **African bush elephant,** 13 feet 2 inches (4 m) at the shoulder. You'd need all day to visit the rest of the museum, but for a highlights tour, begin on the first floor with a pass through the **Kenneth E. Behring Family Hall of Mammals,** with mounted animals from near and far; and the **Hall of Human Origins,** with representations of ancient paintings—handprints, animals, and the like—from around the world. This will lead you into the **Sant Ocean Hall,** with its 45-foot-long (14 m) model of an Atlantic right whale hanging from the ceiling and huge tank containing an Indo-Pacific coral reef alive with up to 74 fishes and other tropical denizens. On the second floor, your first stop should be the dazzling, deep-blue, 45.52-carat **Hope Diamond,** perhaps the world's most famous precious stone. Next, also on this floor, are the **Live Butterfly Pavilion** (*$$, free Tues.; see website for details*) as well as the **Last American Dinosaurs** exhibition. With more time, watch an **IMAX film** (*$$*) or linger in one of the other galleries, **African Voices, Live Insect Zoo, Mummies, Bones,** and **Korea** among them.

National Mall between 9th & 12th Sts., N.W. • tel 202-633-1000 • naturalhistory.si.edu • Metro: Smithsonian

National Gallery of Art

11 One of the world's finest repositories of Western art, the National Gallery is another must-see. The collection is housed in two distinct structures—the **West Building,** a classical pantheon with barrel-vaulted halls designed by John Russell Pope, showcasing masterpieces from the 13th to 19th centuries; and the modern **East Building,** designed by I. M. Pei, displaying masterpieces from the 19th century onward. For those short on time and wanting to see the most famous paintings, begin in the West Building with the **Dutch works,** including Hendrick ter Brugghen's "Bagpipe Player" (1624; Gallery 44). Next up, the **Collection of Italian Art** with a portrait of Ginevra de'Benci (1474/1478; Gallery 06), the only painting by

An African bush elephant greets visitors to the vast National Museum of Natural History, showcasing wonders of the natural world.

Leonardo da Vinci on public view in North America. Next, savor the **French Impressionists,** including Claude Monet's "Woman With a Parasol" (1875; Gallery 85). Then move to the newly renovated East Building and such highlights of **modern art** as Alexander Calder's renowned mobile "Untitled" (1976) and Andy Goldsworthy's "Roof" (2004–2005). Outside, the adjacent **National Gallery of Art Sculpture Garden** offers large installations displayed around a fountain in a lovely setting of trees and flowers. Free jazz concerts take place here on summer Friday evenings, and ice-skating in winter.

West Building: National Mall bet. 4th & 7th Sts., N.W.; East Building: National Mall bet. 3rd & 4th Sts., N.W. ; Sculpture Garden: National Mall bet. 7th & 8th Sts., N.W. • tel 202-737-4215 • nga.gov • Metro: Smithsonian

National Air and Space Museum

See pp. 60–63.

National Mall bet. 4th & 7th Sts., S.W. • tel 202-633-1000 • airandspace.si.edu • Metro: L'Enfant Plaza

National Museum of American History

Some of America's most iconic treasures celebrate everything from the president's role to the Star-Spangled Banner to screen legends in this homage to the nation's history and culture.

Michelle Obama revisits the white silk chiffon gown she wore to the 2009 Inaugural Ball, now part of the "First Ladies" exhibit at the National Museum of American History.

This artifact-filled museum applauds all things great in American history and culture, focusing on such broad themes as transportation, food, the president's role, and innovation. With more than three million items in its collection— as diverse and symbolic as Abraham's Lincoln's top hat, Thomas Edison's light bulbs, and Archie Bunker's armchair—only 3 to 5 percent is on display at any one time. Here are some not-to-be-missed highlights.

NATIONAL MALL

STAR-SPANGLED BANNER

Moved by the sight of the enormous garrison flag flying over Fort McHenry in Baltimore Harbor during the War of 1812, attorney and amateur poet Francis Scott Key scribbled the lyrics to what became the national anthem of the United States. Recently conserved, the same hallowed flag that he viewed is on permanent display as you enter the building from the Mall, on the second floor, with background information on its creator, Mary Pickersgill; the role of the flag in the American psyche; and how the flag was preserved.

DOROTHY'S RUBY SLIPPERS

The **American Stories** gallery on the second floor displays some of America's most iconic artifacts of pop culture, including the ruby slippers worn by Judy Garland in the 1939 movie *The Wizard of Oz.* Look also for the fragment of Plymouth Rock and the original Muppet puppets.

JACQUELINE KENNEDY'S STATE DINNER DRESS

Jackie's elegant yellow silk gown with an overlay of crepe chiffon, a gift from

IN **THE KNOW**

Recent renovation at the museum has sought to bring new relevancy to its interpretation of the American experience. Exhibits explore innovation, the past and present of American democracy, and the role of immigrants in the U.S. melting pot. On display are such prized possessions as Thomas Jefferson's writing desk, on which he wrote the Declaration of Independence.

designer Oleg Cassini, joins first ladies' dresses dating as far back as Martha Washington's silk gown from the early 1780s in the ever popular "First Ladies" exhibit on the third floor center level. In addition to the lovely dresses, the exhibit explores the first ladies' social and political activities.

JULIA CHILD'S KITCHEN

For seven years, in her Cambridge, Massachusetts home, Julia Child gave lessons, tested recipes, and cooked on national television in this very kitchen. In 2001, some 1,200 items and the kitchen were packed and reassembled here. You'll find it in the "FOOD: Transforming the American Table 1950–2000" exhibit on the first floor.

Constitution Ave. bet. 12th & 14th Sts, N.W. • tel 202-633-1000 • americanhistory.si.edu
• Metro: Smithsonian, Federal Triangle

NATIONAL MALL

National Air &
Space Museum

*The evolution of air and space is explored in this magnificent,
ever popular museum on the Mall.*

**Real aircraft are part of what attracts some 9 million visitors annually to this popular
museum, celebrating humankind's achievements in aviation and spaceflight.**

Celebrity air- and spacecraft, intriguing artifacts, interactive exhibits, state-of-
the-art digital displays, and films all tell the story of our fascination with flight,
from the earliest days of hot-air ballooning to the Wright brothers' experiments
with gliders to the current exploration of space. The museum delves into such
intriguing topics as the science of flight, the politics of space exploration, and
the concept of the universe. With 22 galleries, you will need to pace yourself.

CHARLES LINDBERGH'S SPIRIT OF ST. LOUIS

Charles Lindbergh made the first solo flight across the Atlantic in May 1927. You'll find his famous airplane, *Spirit of St. Louis,* hanging from the ceiling in the **Boeing Milestones of Flight Hall,** which highlights aviation's greatest hits just as you enter the museum from the Mall. Here, too, look for Chuck Yeager's Bell X-1 "Glamorous Glennis," the first airplane to fly faster than the speed of sound; the Bell XP-59A, a testing model that proved that turbo-jet-powered flight was possible, paving the way for all American jet aircraft; a replica of *Sputnik I,* the first artificial satellite in history; and the Mercury Friendship 7 capsule in which John Glenn became the first American to orbit the Earth. That said, the most popular exhibit is probably the **Moon rock.** Go ahead, feel free to touch this actual rock brought back from the Moon. Officially known by NASA as piece 84 of sample 70215, and by geologists as dense, aphanitic basalt, this little black stone speaks volumes about what humankind can accomplish when our imaginations take flight.

BOEING 747 NOSE

Enter into the cockpit of a giant Boeing 747 in the nearby **America by Air Gallery,** which explores the history of the nation's commercial aviation. Carrying 400 passengers, the 747 revolutionized long-distance air travel when it entered service in 1970. The exhibit continues its celebration of the evolution of commercial aviation with more aircraft, including a 1926, all-metal, corrugated-aluminum **Ford 5-AT Tri-Motor,** the largest civil airplane at the time (lovingly known as the "tin goose"); and the single-engine **Northrop Alpha,** in which passengers sat in the enclosed space while the pilot remained in the open cockpit.

SUPERMARINE SPITFIRE MK. VII

Also on the first floor, the **World War II Aviation Gallery** displays the legendary Supermarine Spitfire, which helped defend England against the Luftwaffe in the Battle of Britain. Nearby, the Mitsubishi A6M5 Zero was Japan's main naval fighter—used in the Battle of Pearl Harbor as well as kamikaze attacks.

FLIGHT SIMULATORS

Climb inside a motion simulator and see for yourself what it's like to perform 360-degree barrel rolls, or test your skills at air-to-air combat in an F-4 Phantom II jet fighter. Note that a fee is charged for each ride *($$).*

SAVVY **TRAVELER**

The largest and some of the most famous air- and spacecraft are displayed at the Udvar-Hazy Center, a huge Smithsonian annex in nearby Chantilly, Virginia. Here, in a hangar-like facility, you'll find more than 300 aircraft and large space objects, including the Boeing B-29 Superfortress *Enola Gay*, which dropped the first atomic bomb in combat; an Air France Concorde, the first supersonic airliner; and the space shuttle *Discovery*, fresh from its last flight. *14390 Air & Space Museum Pkwy., Chantilly, VA; tel 703-572-4118; airandspace.si.edu; parking: $$$*

■ 1903 WRIGHT FLYER

Examine up close an early Wright flyer and other fabric-covered aircraft in the **Wright Brothers and the Invention of the Aerial Age Gallery** on the second floor, which explores the first decade of flight. Notice the Wright Flyer has skids instead of wheels for landing as well as a sprocket-and-chain transmission system—all evidence of the Wrights' bicycle background. Here, too, look for the rare **Wright St. Clair bicycle,** built in 1898, one of only five that are known to exist. Also on view is a reproduction of the 1900 **Wright glider**, the Wrights' first piloted aircraft, tested out at Kitty Hawk.

■ REAL-LIFE SPACE SUITS

One of the museum's mind-blowing exhibits is the real-life space suits worn by Apollo astronauts on the Moon. These can be ogled at the **Apollo to the Moon Gallery** on the second floor. This exhibit, filled with artifacts related to the Apollo and earlier missions, takes a look at the challenge of putting a man on the Moon—a feat made possible only with the help of half a million people, thousands of technical innovations, and seemingly infinite resourcefulness. Among the other artifacts to look for: an F-1 rocket engine, used during Apollo lunar landing missions; and a lunar roving vehicle, which could carry two astronauts and all of their equipment up to 57 miles (92 km).

■ HUBBLE TEST TELESCOPE

The rivalry between the Soviets and the Americans following World War II fueled a competition to outpace each other into space—a race that led to the rapid advancement of technology. Some of the results are on display in the **Space Race Gallery** on the second floor, including the Hubble Test Telescope, a full-scale mock-up built in 1975 and used to conduct feasibility studies before launching the real telescope in 1990.

Rockets, missiles, and the huge Skylab Orbital Workshop attest to the race to space.

■ IMAX MOVIES

The museum's popular IMAX theaters, complete with next-generation laser projection and sound systems, comfy seating, and enormous screens measuring up to six stories tall, are one of the museum's top highlights. For that reason, be sure to purchase tickets online ahead of time, or immediately upon entering the museum. Past shows have included "Journey to Space" and "D-Day: Normandy." Note that all shows charge an entrance fee *($$$)*.

600 Independence Ave., S.W. • tel 202- 633-2214 • airandspace.si.edu • Metro: L'Enfant Plaza

Cherry Blossoms

Every spring the city waits with bated breath for the blossoming of the famous, 3,000-plus Yoshino cherry trees along the Tidal Basin. It's never guaranteed exactly when they'll peak—April 4 is the average. But suddenly, seemingly overnight, everyone's mood notably lightens as these delicate little flowers, a gift from the Japanese in the early 20th century, explode into a billowy world of white and pink.

The undeniable seasonal beauty of masses of soft pink petals proves an irresistible draw for visitors to the Tidal Basin, whether viewed from the water (above) or beneath the boughs (opposite). The city's month-long festival honors the continuing friendship between the United States and Japan.

The First Trees

The idea for Washington's cherry trees can be traced to Eliza Scidmore, a late 19th-century travel writer who so admired the flowering cherry trees in Japan that she lobbied park officials to plant similar ones in her hometown of Washington, D.C. They weren't interested. About a quarter century later, botanist David Fairchild experimented with flowering cherry trees and planted some around the town of Chevy Chase, Maryland. These inspired First Lady Helen Taft to place some around a drab area along the Potomac River. In a gesture of friendship, the mayor of Tokyo, Japan, sent trees as a gift—twice, as the first arrived diseased. The second batch of 3,000 were planted along the Tidal Basin in March 1912, with Mrs. Taft placing the first one.

Blossom Viewing

The Japanese have turned *sakura* viewing into an art—called *hanami*—which involves long strolls as well as songs and picnics beneath the blooms. In D.C., visitors can experience hanami by paddleboat (*tidalbasinpaddleboats.com*) for a waterborne view, or by bicycle, available for rent from Capitol Bikeshare (*capitalbikeshare.com*). To avoid peak crowds, try visiting the Tidal Basin early or late in the day.

National Cherry Blossom Festival

The National Cherry Blossom Festival (*national cherryblossomfestival.org*) has taken place since 1927, today drawing more than 1.5 million visitors with hundreds of mostly free events and activities offered over four weekends. Highlights include the parade on Constitution Avenue (*between 7th & 17th Sts., N.W.*), with its elaborate floats, entertainers, and marching bands; the Sakura Matsuri–Japanese Street Festival on Pennsylvania Avenue (*between 9th & 14th Sts., N.W.*); and the Blossom Kite Festival on the Washington Monument grounds.

BEYOND **THE TIDAL BASIN**

Here are some other beautiful, lesser known places for *hanami:*

East Potomac Park More cherry trees near the Tidal Basin, along the Potomac River and Washington Channel. *nps.gov*

Kenwood A Bethesda, Maryland, neighborhood that offers an excellent Plan B. *visitmontgomery.com*

U.S. National Arboretum Many different varieties of cherries, blooming at different times. *usna.usda.gov*

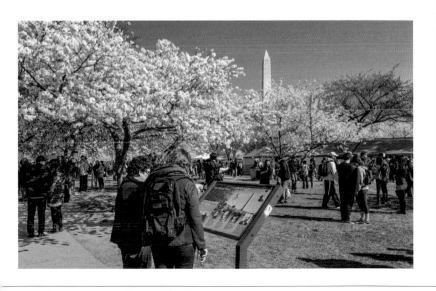

Free Entertainment

Washington is famous for its free admission to some of the world's greatest museums. A lesser known fact is that there are many free cultural events as well, especially throughout the summer. From big bands to big screens, cool jazz to contemporary theater, here are some of the best.

■ SUMMER MILITARY BAND CONCERTS

Get into the patriotic spirit with the music of talented U.S. military bands performing at outdoor concerts throughout the summer. Catch the **U.S. Navy Band** (*www.navyband.navy.mil*) at 8 p.m. Mondays at the U.S. Capitol or at 7:30 p.m. Tuesdays at the U.S. Navy Memorial. The **U.S. Air Force Band** (*www.usafband.af.mil*) plays at 8 p.m. Tuesdays at the U.S. Capitol; 8 p.m. Wednesdays at the National Sylvan Theater, in front of the Washington Monument; and 8 p.m. Fridays at the U.S. Air Force Memorial in Arlington. The **U.S. Marine Band** (*www.marineband.marines.mil*) plays at 8 p.m. Wednesdays at the U.S. Capitol and 8:45 p.m. Fridays at the Marine Barracks (*8th & I Sts., S.W.*). And finally, the rousing **U.S. Army Band** (*www.usarmyband.com*) performs before the U.S. Capitol on Fridays at 8 p.m.

■ A CAPITOL FOURTH

Washington offers many ways to celebrate the Fourth of July, including the televised "A Capitol Fourth" concert on the West Lawn of the U.S. Capitol building—an evening of music capped by fireworks over glowing monuments. It's all free, but people start lining up for entry well before the 8 p.m. start time.

National Mall • nps.gov/nama • Metro: Smithsonian

■ JAZZ IN THE GARDEN

On sultry Friday evenings between Memorial Day and Labor Day, bebop to a wide variety of jazz amid giant sculptures at the National Gallery of Art's Sculpture Garden. Bands play between 5 p.m. and 8:30 p.m. Purchase food (and sangria!) from the Pavilion Café or bring your own picnic basket.

National Gallery of Art Sculpture Garden, Constitution Ave. & 7th St., N.W. • tel 202-289-3360 • nga.gov • Metro: Smithsonian

The U. S. Navy Band performs in front of the United States Capitol as part of the group's free summer evening concert series.

■ MILLENNIUM STAGE

Perhaps one of the greatest finds in Washington is the Kennedy Center's Millennium Stage, where local, national, and international artists present music, dance, and theater at 6 p.m. For free! You don't need a ticket, but seating is limited and available only on a first-come, first-served basis. Check the website to see who's performing next. You can also join a free guided tour.

John F. Kennedy Center for the Performing Arts, 2700 F St., N.W. • tel 202-467-4600 or 800-444-1324 • kennedy-center.org • Metro: Foggy Bottom–GWU

■ THE YARDS PARK AT CAPITOL RIVERFRONT

Enjoy live music on Friday evenings at the lovely waterfront setting of The Yards Park (see sidebar p. 72) along the Anacostia River, near Nationals Park baseball stadium. Spread a blanket on grassy open space and purchase a ready-made picnic at one of the nearby restaurants—or bring your own. Check the website to see which band is on tap—the variety ranges from reggae to country to indie.

The Yards Park, Capitol Riverfront, 35 Water St., S.E. • tel 202-465-7080 • yardspark.org • Metro: Navy Yard–Ballpark

Capitol Hill

The seat of the world's foremost democratic power rises on a swell of land on the National Mall's eastern edge—a site that civil planner Pierre-Charles L'Enfant described as a "pedestal waiting for a superstructure." Architect William Thornton designed the white-marble, Pantheon-like dome flanked by symmetrical wings of the Senate and the House, and George Washington himself laid the cornerstone in 1793. The Capitol remained the only government building on "the Hill" until the late 19th century, when it was joined by the Library of Congress's Jefferson Building, and Daniel H. Burnham's Union Station and Washington City Post Office. In the 1930s the U.S. Supreme Court, Folger Shakespeare Library, and more were added to the mix. The surrounding Capitol Hill neighborhood, with its historic row houses, is a lovely place to stroll, especially in springtime. Eastern Market comes alive on weekends with outdoor markets, while Barracks Row (Eighth Street) has blossomed with trendy restaurants and bars.

◐ **Representations
of past patriots and
heroes, chosen by
the individual states,
adorn the U.S. Capitol's
two-story National
Statuary Hall.**

Capitol Hill

Discover the regal, marble-clad seat of the nation's power—and its friendly residential side as well.

8 Barracks Row (Eighth Street)
(see p. 77) One of the city's newest hot spots, this five-block streetscape south of Pennsylvania Ave., S.E., offers fun eateries plus a historic self-guided walking tour.

7 Eastern Market (see pp. 76–77) A great place to find farm-fresh makings for breakfast or lunch, this bustling market comes alive on weekends with outdoor stalls purveying local produce, flowers, and arts and crafts. Continue down 7th St., N.E., to Pennsylvania Ave., S.E., turn left, and cross Pennsylvania to 8th St., S.E.

1 Union Station (see p. 72)
Grab a cup of coffee at this imposing neoclassical train station and enjoy its lovely architecture. Then walk uphill on Delaware Ave, N.E., to the U.S. Capitol. The visitor center is on your left, at the back of the building.

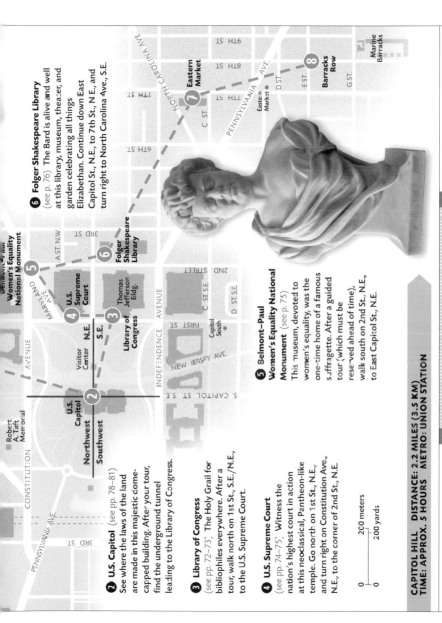

2 U.S. Capitol (see pp. 78–81)
See where the laws of the land are made in this majestic dome-capped building. After your tour, find the underground tunnel leading to the Library of Congress.

3 Library of Congress
(see pp. 72–73) The Holy Grail for bibliophiles everywhere. After a tour, walk north on 1st St., S.E./N.E., to the U.S. Supreme Court.

4 U.S. Supreme Court
(see pp. 74–75) Witness the nation's highest court in action at this neoclassical, Pantheon-like temple. Go north on 1st St., N.E., and turn right on Constitution Ave., N.E., to the corner of 2nd St., N.E

5 Belmont–Paul Women's Equality National Monument (see p.75)
This museum, devoted to women's equality, was the one-time home of a famous suffragette. After a guided tour (which must be reserved ahead of time), walk south on 2nd St., N.E., to East Capitol St., N.E.

6 Folger Shakespeare Library
(see p. 76) The Bard is alive and well at this library, museum, theater, and garden celebrating all things Elizabethan. Continue down East Capitol St., N.E., to 7th St., N.E., and turn right to North Carolina Ave., S.E.

CAPITOL HILL   DISTANCE: 2.2 MILES (3.5 KM)
TIME: APPROX. 5 HOURS   METRO: UNION STATION

0   200 meters
0   200 yards

CAPITOL HILL

IN **THE KNOW**

The Yards Park, a 15- to 20-minute walk away from the Hill, is the perfect place to relax. A revitalized stretch of land along the Anacostia River, it has a boardwalk, fountains, and a terraced lawn where bands play on summer Friday evenings (see p. 67). It's part of the larger Yards project, which offers restaurants and bars galore and—not too far away—Nationals Park, home of the MLB team the Washington Nationals. *yardspark.org*

CAPITOL HILL

Union Station

1 Start your day with coffee at this majestic train station, modeled in part after the Baths of Caraculla and Diocletian and the Arch of Rome—and definitely worth visiting just for its architecture. Grand arches give way to the triumphal, echoing **Main Hall,** where 36 larger-than-life Roman legionnaires preside on the gallery level. A barrel-vaulted ceiling with gold-leaf coffers soars above the station's bustle; more than 90,000 visitors pass through here every day, some stopping at the 100-plus specialty shops and restaurants. It's undergoing a major, 8.5-billion-dollar expansion and redevelopment plan, complete with a hotel and parks. The website's "Union Station Tour" app includes a self-guided tour and an interactive scavenger hunt.

2 West/40 Massachusetts Ave., N.E. • tel 202-289-1908 • unionstationdc.com • Metro: Union Station

U.S. Capitol

2 See pp. 78–81.

East Capitol St., N.E., & 1st St., S.E. • tel 202-226-8000 • visitthecapitol.gov • book tours through your Congressperson, online, or obtain first-come, first-served tickets at the visitor center • Metro: Union Station, Capitol South

Library of Congress

3 Truly a glorious temple of learning, the Italian Renaissance–style Thomas Jefferson building of the Library of Congress—the main building—dazzles the eye with its opulent yet tasteful cornucopia of sculpture, mural mosaics, and architectural flourishes. The world's largest library, the Library of Congress has 160 million items, including President Washington's 1789 first inaugural address; the first map to name America, the Waldseemüller map; and 2,100 baseball cards dating from 1887 to 1914. You can take an organized

Allegorical statues representing civilization and learning, as well as great thinkers of the past, watch over today's scholars from the galleries of the Main Reading Room, Library of Congress.

tour of the Jefferson Building or pick up a self-guided tour brochure at the visitor center just inside the west side's ground level entrance. At the very least, don't miss the gilded **Great Hall** on the first floor, where you'll feel as if you've entered a Mediterranean palazzo. Nearby, two Library treasures rest behind glass cases: the Giant Bible of Mainz and the Gutenberg Bible, both made in Germany in the mid-1450s. Then climb the stairs to peer down into the historic **Main Reading Room,** whose 250 desks are arranged under a dome 160 feet (49 m) above the floor. With extra time, peruse the second floor's side galleries, featuring permanent and rotating exhibitions of American history and culture. Want a closer look at the Library's offerings? Use your driver's license or passport to obtain your own library card. Even if you don't use it, it makes for a great souvenir.

Thomas Jefferson Bldg., 10 1st St., S.E. • tel 202-707-8000 • loc.gov • Metro: Capitol South, Union Station

U.S. Supreme Court

4 In this imposing neoclassical building, the nation's highest tribunal hears cases involving the Constitution or the nation's laws. It's here that the nation's most famous and influential decisions have been handed down. From the front plaza, you enter on the ground floor, where **exhibitions** delve into the court's history and architecture—you'll see Chief Justice John Marshall's bench chair (used between 1819 and 1835), a calendar depicting the first month of action (October 1935), and models providing insight into the symbolism behind the East and West Pediments. Crane your neck up at the five-story, marble-and-bronze **spiral staircases,** designed by the building's architect, Cass Gilbert, and watch the introductory 24-minute film. Then climb the majestic stairs to the **Great Hall** on the first floor and its long line of busts depicting

The U.S. Supreme Court's west facade proclaims the guiding principle, "Equal Justice Under Law."

former chief justices. At the end of the hall lies the actual **courtroom,** which you can look into when the court is not in session. Docents offer lectures here every hour on the half-hour, covering the judicial functions of the Supreme Court as well as the building's history and architecture. When the court is in session *(Oct.–mid-May),* you can listen to oral arguments by lining up on the Front Plaza; the schedule is on the website. Note there is a line for those who just want to hear a three-minute sample of the case.

1st St., N.E. • tel 202-479-3000 • supremecourt.gov • closed Sat.–Sun. • Metro: Capitol South, Union Station

Belmont–Paul Women's Equality National Monument

5 Robert Sewall built this two-story brick house in 1799 and later rented it to Albert Gallatin, secretary of the treasury, from 1801 to 1813 (he probably penned the Louisiana Purchase here). But it's perhaps most famous for being the staging ground for feminist education and social change. Multimillionaire socialite and suffragette Alva Belmont helped purchase the house in 1929 for the National Women's Party, a nonpartisan organization that lobbied for women's rights for more than 60 years. Alice Stokes Paul, lifelong activist for women's equality and author of the proposed Equal Rights Amendment, was the house's primary resident for 40 years. The museum has recently been brought to greater prominence, after President Obama designated the house a national monument in 2016. Among the sepia photographs and fading banners, you'll also find personal items of two icons of the women's suffrage movement, Susan B. Anthony and Elizabeth Cady Stanton. Call ahead for a tour or reserve a spot online.

144 Constitution Ave., N.E. • tel 202-546-1210 • nps.gov/bepa, sewallbelmont.org • by guided tour only: Thurs.–Sat. • $$ • Metro: Capitol South, Union Station

GOOD **EATS**

■ MR. HENRY'S RESTAURANT

Serving the Hill since 1966, this hole-in-the-wall burger joint offers up creative sandwiches. **601 Pennsylvania Ave., S.E., tel 202-546-8412, $**

■ MONTMARTRE

A delightful French bistro with outdoor seating. **327 7th St., S.E., tel 202-544-1244, closed Mon. $$**

■ TED'S BULLETIN RESTAURANT

Comfort food with a twist: peanut butter bacon burgers, grilled cheese-and-tomato soup, and adult milkshakes. **505 8th St., S.E., tel 202-544-8337, $$**

CAPITOL HILL

Folger Shakespeare Library

6 This unique library, dedicated in 1932, holds the world's largest collection of William Shakespeare's printed works from the 16th century to present day, plus a world-famous collection of prints, manuscripts, and books. Before you enter, notice the marble, art deco–inspired, neoclassical exterior, adorned with nine bas-relief scenes from Shakespearean plays. Inside, you are greeted by Shakespeare's Tudor world, highlighted by the oak-paneled **Great Hall.** Changing exhibits in this large room showcase some of the library's vast collection, always focusing on some theme relevant to the life and times of Shakespeare, such as the role of women in medicine. Look in the hall's southeastern corner for the **Shakespeare First Folio,** the first collected edition of Shakespeare's plays and the only source for 18 of his plays—without which these dramatic treasures would have been lost forever. Through the door at the Great Hall's eastern end, you enter into the foyer leading to the **Folger Theatre,** a replication of the Elizabethan Globe Theatre. Feel free to walk around and take a look—though it's definitely worth returning in the evening to see the stage in action. Guided tours are available of the Tudor-style **Paster Reading Room** (pull aside the curtains from the Great Hall for a peek), complete with a 16th-century Jacobean table. The bust of Shakespeare on the east wall is one of two approved likenesses. Outside, an enchanting **Elizabethan flower and herb garden** is filled with plants popular during Shakespeare's lifetime; it can be seen only by guided tour from April through October.

201 E. Capitol St., S.E. • tel 202-544-4600 • folger.edu • see website for docent-led and special tour schedules • Metro: Union Station, South Capitol

Eastern Market

7 Since 1873, Eastern Market has been the residential heart of Capitol Hill, a draw for locals and visitors alike. Tuesday through Sunday, local merchants at the indoor **South Hall Market** purvey all the makings for a gourmet picnic: wonderful meats, seafood, cheese, produce, baked goods, and more. Or if you want

Leafy streets, outdoor dining, and a friendly atmosphere add to the appeal of the Capitol Hill neighborhood around Eastern Market.

something made on the spot, line up at the **Market Lunch** counter *(tel 202-547-8444).* On weekends, there's a bustling outdoor farmer's market; an arts and crafts market and antique dealers add to the mix.

225 7th St., S.E. • tel 202-698-5253 • easternmarket-dc.org • closed Mon. • Metro: Eastern Market

Barracks Row (Eighth Street)

8 After a long day, Washingtonians in the know head to this lively culinary scene that has injected new life into the city's oldest commercial corridor. Its name derives from the nearby U.S. Marine Corps Barracks, which it has long served, along with the nearby Washington Navy Yard. **Cultural Tourism DC** *(culturaltourismdc.org)* offers a self-guided heritage walking tour of the neighborhood, clearly marked by 16 poster-size signs along the way. Otherwise, this is a great place to sip a cocktail, linger over creative cuisine, and plan your next move.

8th St. bet. D & I Sts., S.E. • tel 202-544-3188 • barracksrow.org • Metro: Eastern Market

U.S. Capitol

*The center of America's political power rises majestically
on a hill in neoclassical splendor.*

CAPITOL HILL

The U.S. Capitol's dome-topped center building is flanked by two wings hosting the chambers of Congress: the House of Representatives to the south and the Senate to the north.

Visible from vantage points across Washington, the regal U.S. Capitol building serves as a constant reminder of the nation's democratic foundation. For it is here, in its hallowed halls, that Congress meets and the many voices of the union are brought together to discuss and create the laws of the land. Designed by Dr. William Thornton in 1793 and partially burned by the British during the War of 1812, the Capitol was fully restored in 1863 and is crowned by the 19.5-foot-tall (6 m) bronze statue of "Freedom."

■ U.S. CAPITOL VISITOR CENTER

Begin at the underground U.S. Capitol Visitor Center, which serves as the gateway for all tours. Be sure to take some time to stroll through **Emancipation Hall** on the lower level, which offers insightful exhibits incorporating original documents and interactive videos—don't miss the 11-foot-high (3 m) cross section of the Capitol dome at one-twentieth its size, both inside and out. At your allocated tour time, line up as directed. The tour starts with a 13-minute film explaining the history and role of Congress.

■ ORIGINAL FRONT DOOR

Starting on the building's south side, you'll enter via the Capitol's original front door, dating from 1793. Just inside, in the **Senate Vestibule,** Corinthian columns topped with corncobs are among the Capitol's oldest artifacts.

■ OLD SUPREME COURT

The U.S. Supreme Court, which originally met only twice a year, convened in this room between 1810 and 1860. The Dred Scott case was one of the most notable decisions made here. Note the number of chairs available for spectators. In the fledgling city, watching a Supreme Court prosecution was a high form of entertainment— and a

great way to get caught up on the news of the day.

■ CRYPT

The nation's forefathers hoped that George and Martha Washington would be buried in the Capitol building, and a special place was designed for their final resting place. But they had other plans—they preferred to be laid to rest at their home in Mount Vernon. Today, the tomb remains empty, and the crypt now contains some of the **National Statuary Hall Collection**—you'll find the first 13 Colonies represented here. The beautiful sandstone columns were carved by enslaved people, as was much of the original Capitol building.

■ ROTUNDA

A trip up the stairs leads to the large and grandiose Rotunda. This glorious domed room is where Congress comes to celebrate— whether it's both sides of Congress convening to toast a new bill, receiving an esteemed visitor or head of state, or honoring an outstanding American upon their death. Only 33 people have lain in state here since the 1850s, including Rosa Parks (the only woman), Ronald Reagan, Abraham Lincoln, and John F. Kennedy. On the walls, four giant panels by John

SAVVY **TRAVELER**

Be advised that passes are required to tour the Capitol building. Book in advance online (visitthecapitol.gov)**, through the offices of your senators or representative, or through the Office of Visitor Services** (tel 202/226-8000)**. A limited number of same-day passes are issued from the visitor center's lower level. Separate gallery passes are required to watch the House or Senate in session— you can request these in advance or in person from your senator or representative; international visitors should stop by the Appointments Desk at the visitor center. In addition, some congressional offices offer staff-led tours to constituent groups of up to 15 people, or they can help you book a general tour. If you just want to view the visitor center exhibits or have lunch at the restaurant, passes are not required. Note that drinks, food, and aerosol containers are not allowed in the Capitol building. Check the website for additional details as well as policies on etiquette and security.**

Trumbull depict the American Revolution; with four other panels by various artists illustrating the themes of exploration and settlement (including Pocahontas's baptism before her marriage to John Rolfe). Be sure to look up at the dome's ceiling, where a fresco entitled "The Apotheosis of Washington," painted in 1865 by the Italian–American artist Constantino Brumidi, shows a dreamy, cloud-filled scene where George Washington is joined by 13 women symbolizing the 13 Colonies and American democracy. Among the many state statues in this room is one donated by Congress honoring the National Women's Party depicting Susan B. Anthony, Elizabeth Stanton, and Lucretia Mott—and there's room for one more woman because, as the sculptor believes, the story is still ongoing.

■ NATIONAL STATUARY HALL
This beautiful Greek Revival hall— one of the earliest examples in America—served as the House of Representatives between 1807 and 1857. Bronze plaques mark the spots where various representatives sat, including Abraham Lincoln and John Quincy Adams. Alas, the smooth, curved ceiling created poor acoustics, making it nearly impossible to understand debates as well as creating some "whispering spots," such as at Adams's desk, where you may clearly hear a soft voice from many yards away. The House moved to its present chamber in the House wing in 1857, and this room became the official National Statuary Hall. Beginning in 1864, every state was invited to send two statues to be displayed here—the only rules

"The Apotheosis of Washington" appears shrouded in clouds during a recent renovation.

being that the person must be dead, and the statue had to be marble or bronze. Today, one-third of Congress's collection of statues is found here, including ones of **Father Junipero Serra** (California), **Henry Clay** (Kentucky), and **Robert E. Lee** (Virginia).

◼ GALLERIES

A separate pass is required to visit the Galleries (see sidebar opposite), where you can look down on either the House or Senate floors and view for yourself the long and complicated process of lawmaking.

◼ U.S. CAPITOL GROUNDS

The Capitol sits on 58.8 acres (24 ha) of landscaped grounds designed by renowned landscape architect Frederick Law Olmsted. Take a stroll to enjoy the building from all angles, then follow pathways from its south side, down the hill to the **U.S. Botanic Garden** (see p. 156). Cross in front of the **Capitol Reflecting Pool**, taking note of the statue of General Grant (the nation's largest equestrian statue), before climbing up the other side. You'll come across pocket gardens, memorial trees, hidden statues, and plenty of benches.

East Capitol St., N.E., & 1st St., S.E. • tel 202-226-8000 • visitthecapitol.gov • Metro: Union Station

Capital City

Washington, D.C., was founded in 1790 to serve exclusively as the fledgling nation's capital, where the president would live and where the laws of the land would be made and upheld. Topped by the majestic Capitol building and dotted with various congressional offices, much of Capitol Hill is devoted to making legislation. But its reach extends far beyond.

Above: This 1922 photograph shows how Washington's boundary stones—marking the perimeter of the District of Columbia—have long been worthy reminders of the Founding Fathers' ideas for the nation's capital. Opposite: A stylized "View of Washington City" circa 1852. A larger Capitol dome was completed in 1866.

Why Washington?

Alexander Hamilton wanted the new government to be located in the North. Thomas Jefferson wanted the capital within reach of the agricultural South. George Washington made the final decision—a 100-square-mile (259 sq km) area carved out of Maryland and Virginia near his home at Mount Vernon. The compromise offered an accessible trade route to the western frontier via the Potomac and Ohio River Valleys.

L'Enfant Hired

The city's original plan was devised by Frenchman Pierre-Charles L'Enfant, who came to America to fight the Revolutionary War. He ended up designing the Capital City on what was, essentially, a clean slate of undulating, plantation-dotted landscape. Using European models with a dash of American ideals, he placed Congress on the highest point (where in Europe the leader's house would be) with wide avenues radiating beyond, punctuated by important buildings and attractive squares and parks. Centerpiece of it all: The 400-foot-wide (122 m), tree-lined "grand avenue" that later became the National Mall.

CAPITOL HILL

L'Enfant Fired

But L'Enfant's perfectionist traits led to his being fired. Eventually the city's surveyor, Andrew Ellicott, took over with a plan based on L'Enfant's vision, but with the compromises he refused to consider (the waterfall cascading off Capitol Hill, for example, was scratched). However, the capital remained incomplete for more than a century; even after the Civil War there was talk of moving the capital to Philadelphia or the Midwest.

At Long Last

The McMillan Commission was formed in 1902, taking to task the completion of the Capital City. Still within the confines of L'Enfant's original plan, they built parks and reclaimed land to make space for the Lincoln and Jefferson Memorials. At long last, elegant Washington began to emerge, an impression that remains to this day.

BOUNDARY
STONES

When the original perimeter of Washington, D.C., was surveyed, the 10-by-10-mile (16 x 16 km) outline was marked with sandstone cairns one mile (1.6 km) apart—supervised by George Washington himself. The nation's oldest federal monuments, 37 of the 40 stones remain in place to this day. They are a popular treasure hunt for walkers and bikers, and a great way to delve into D.C.'s varied neighborhoods. Some are obvious, others not so. That's what makes making a boundary-stone quest so fun!
boundarystones.org

Watering Holes

Washington has a long tradition of watering holes frequented by politicians and everyone else in need of a place to unwind after work, discuss a deal, and talk the talk. And, as every Hill intern knows, many bars offer well-priced happy hours, complete with free or inexpensive snacks.

■ THE MONOCLE

The location as the closest eatery to the Senate side of the Capitol virtually guarantees politico-sightings. (Hint: Look for the lapel button worn by members of Congress.) It opened in 1960, when regular customers Richard M. Nixon and John F. Kennedy were battling for the presidency. Auto-graphed photographs hanging on the walls span decades of Hill history. It's a restaurant, too, serving an all-American menu of burgers, steaks, and seafood.

107 D St., N.E. • tel 202-546-4488
• themonocle.com • Metro: Union Station

■ HAWK 'N' DOVE

Established in 1967, this longtime Capitol Hill favorite attracts locals, congressional staffers, and the occasional political celebrity. A relatively recent renovation has done away with the warren of hidden rooms, opening up the space with a contemporary look. Burgers, sandwiches, and beer dominate the menu.

329 Pennsylvania Ave., S.E. • tel 202-547-0030
• hawkanddovedc.com • Metro: Capitol South

■ POV

You don't get much better views than from the rooftop balcony of the W hotel's POV (point of view) bar—a bird's-eye angle of the White House to one side, the monument-dotted Mall on the other. On a clear day, if you squint to the west, you can just make out the eternal flame flickering off in the Arlington National Cemetery, beyond the Lincoln Memorial. Owned by W Hotels and Resorts, the former Hotel Washington offers cushioned sofas, lounge chairs, and an imaginative drinks menu. The only downside: the long lines of crowds waiting to get in.

W Washington D.C. , 515 15th St., N.W.
• tel 202-661-2400 • wwashingtondc.com
• Metro: Metro Center

Where deals go down: The back bar at Old Ebbitt Grill, site of many political assignations

■ OLD EBBITT GRILL

A favorite haunt of former Presidents Ulysses S. Grant, Grover Cleveland, and Theodore Roosevelt, this D.C. staple was founded in 1856 and is Washington's oldest, most historic saloon (though the current building dates from 1983). It remains a popular spot for D.C. celebrities, journalists, and politicians. Always crowded, the large restaurant offers a menu full of burgers, grilled fish, and a notable selection of oysters. The walrus head hanging in the bar is reputed to have been bagged by Theodore Roosevelt.

675 15th St., N.W. • tel 202-347-4800 • ebbitt.com • Metro: Metro Center

■ ROUND ROBIN BAR

The bar of choice for presidential discussions—whether you're a president-elect, politician, lobbyist, reporter, or general onlooker—ever since it opened in the Willard hotel in 1850. Mark Twain and Walt Whitman are among those who have lingered here through the years. The bartender, Jim Hewes, is nearly as famous as the hotel; he's been tending bar here for more than 30 years. The adjacent Scotch Bar is also popular.

Willard InterContinental Washington, 1401 Pennsylvania Ave., N.W. • tel 202-628-9100 • washington.intercontinental.com • Metro: Metro Center

Downtown

Just north of Pennsylvania Avenue, N.W., between 14th and 7th Streets, and reaching as far north as Louisiana and Massachusetts Avenues, N.W., Washington's downtown area booms with the bustle of everyday urban life. This corner of the city suffered great devastation during the 1968 riots after the assassination of Martin Luther King, Jr. In the following years, area crime skyrocketed as buildings fell into decay. But downtown is looking up: Revitalization has come to stay, kick-started with the arrival of the MCI Center (now Verizon Center) sports and events complex in 1997—home to the Washington Wizards NBA basketball team and Washington Capitals NHL team, as well as world-class entertainment events. Here, in a vibrant area dubbed Penn Quarter, über-trendy restaurants, boutiques, art galleries, and theaters thrive. Amid all this buzz, don't overlook several excellent museums, including the Newseum, Smithsonian American Art Museum and National Portrait Gallery, and the ever popular International Spy Museum.

⬤ Four tiers of arcades face two sets of huge columns within the light-filled Great Hall of the National Building Museum, built to resemble a vast Italian palazzo.

Downtown

Located in the Northwest quadrant, to the north of the National Mall and the broad swath of Pennsylvania Avenue, Washington's vibrant downtown area booms with restaurants, shops, theaters, and galleries.

DOWNTOWN

❶ Freedom Plaza (see p. 90)
Look down to see the inlaid bronze map depicting L'Enfant's original city plan on this granite plaza. Then set your sights on the Capitol as you walk down Pennsylvania Ave., N.W., to 6th St., N.W.

❷ Newseum (see pp. 96–99)
Try your hand at being a news reporter at this popular museum covering all things news. Next, cross the street and turn right on Constitution Ave., N.W.

National Mus. of Women in the Arts

NEW YORK AVE

Metro Center

G ST.

14TH STREET N.W.

13TH ST.

12TH ST.

F ST.

National Theatre

Warner Theatre

PENN. AVE. N.

E ST.

Freedom Plaza ❶

Federal Triangle

C Po Of

❸ National Archives (see pp. 90–91) Pay your respects to the nation's most important documents—the Constitution and Declaration of Independence among them. Continue on Constitution Ave., N.W., to 9th St. N.W. Turn right, then left on E St. N.W., then right on 10th St., N.W.

**DOWNTOWN   DISTANCE: 2.2 MILES (3.5 KM)
TIME: APPROX. 12 HOURS   METRO: METRO CENTER**

8 Woolly Mammoth Theatre
(see p. 95) End the day with an edgy theater experience.

7 National Building Museum
(see p. 95) An imposing building with fascinating exhibits related to architecture. Backtrack on F St., N.W., returning to Penn Quarter.

6 International Spy Museum
(see pp. 94–95) A fascinating look into the world of spies—they might be closer than you think! Continue east on F St., N.W., for 2.5 blocks.

5 Smithsonian American Art Museum and National Portrait Gallery
(see pp. 93–94) Albert Bierstadt, Mary Cassatt, and John La Farge are among the American artists applauded in this bright, beautifully curated art museum paired with a portrait gallery notable for its lineup of U.S. presidents. Cross F St., N.W.

4 Ford's Theatre N.H.S. (see pp. 91–93) Visit the still active theater where Lincoln was killed, as well as its insightful museum. Continue up 10th St., N.W., to F St., N.W., and turn right for 1.5 blocks.

Freedom Plaza

1 This modernist granite plaza, built in 1980 and overlooked by an equestrian statue of Polish military commander Casimir Pulaski, includes an inlaid map of L'Enfant's original plan for the city. Renamed in honor of Martin Luther King, Jr., who wrote much of his "I Have a Dream" speech nearby, its grand, sweeping view down Pennsylvania Avenue all the way to the Capitol makes a telegenic backdrop to the various political protests that often convene here.

Pennsylvania Ave., bet. 13th & 14th Sts., N.W. • tel 202-619-7222 • nps.gov • Metro: Federal Triangle, Metro Center

Newseum

2 See pp. 96–99.

555 Pennsylvania Ave., N.W. • tel 202-292-6100 • newseum.org • $$$$$ • Metro: Archives–Navy Memorial–Penn Quarter, Judiciary Square

National Archives

3 The Charters of Freedom—the **Declaration of Independence, Constitution,** and **Bill of Rights**—are the star attractions in this grand neoclassical edifice, designed in 1935 for the express purpose of housing America's most revered documents. More than 12 billion paper records dating back to 1774 are preserved here (and billions more recent electronic records as well), though most are kept behind the scenes. Enter from Constitution Avenue, where the interactive **"Records of Rights"** exhibit addresses how the ideals enshrined in the original Charters of Freedom did not initially apply to all Americans—African Americans, women, Native Americans, and immigrants among them. Upstairs, in the hushed silence of the **Rotunda,** the Charters of Freedom are displayed in state-of-the-art cases. New York artist Barry Faulkner painted the two large murals hanging above the documents: "The Constitution" on the right, with George Washington in his white cape the obvious centerpiece; and "The Declaration of Independence" on the left (the figures for both are identified in nearby charts). On this floor, too, the fascinating

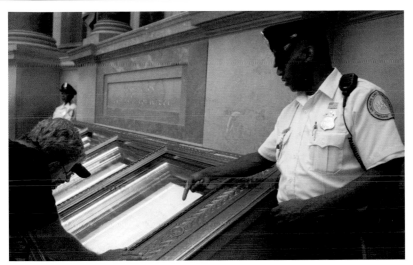

The nation's Charters of Freedom are fiercely guarded at the National Archives in specially designed aluminum and titanium cases, with the documents surrounded by an inert gas.

and enormous **"Public Vaults"** exhibit delves deeply into the stacks, with videos, photographs, maps, and interpretive panels on display, as well as some of the archives' more interesting documents—from George Washington's handwritten letters to Abraham Lincoln's wartime telegrams to original D-Day footage.

Constitution Ave. bet. 7th & 9th Sts., N.W. • tel 866-272-6272 • archives.gov
• Metro: Archives–Navy Memorial–Penn Quarter

Ford's Theatre National Historic Site

4 History was forever changed on the evening of April 14, 1865, when John Wilkes Booth shot President Abraham Lincoln in the Presidential Box of this theater, five days after Lee's surrender at Appomattox. The theater remained closed for more than a hundred years; the National Park Service acquired it in 1933, restored it to its original 1865 splendor in the 1960s, and renovated it once again in

2009. Today's visitors enter the museum downstairs, among absorbing exhibits exploring Lincoln's life. Look for such noteworthy artifacts as the .44-caliber derringer pistol Booth used in the shooting, Booth's escape diary, and the frock coat Lincoln was wearing on that fateful evening. Then climb the stairs to the Dress Circle and Balcony, overlooking the stage and the flag-draped **Presidential Box,** which has been authentically re-created with red velvet wallpaper, plush seats, and the original settee. In addition to the Park Service tours, the theater hosts a full program of contemporary American plays.

Continue your tour across the street to the **Petersen House,** where Lincoln was frantically carried as his life slipped away. Peek into the parlor where Mary Todd Lincoln nervously paced through the night; the back parlor where Edwin Stanton, Lincoln's secretary of war, began investigating the murder; and the bedroom where Lincoln died. From here, an elevator whisks you to more exhibits

The Friendship Arch stands at the entrance to D.C.'s Chinatown, established in the 1930s.

on three separate floors, describing Lincoln's world. Timed tickets are free, but reservations are required; visit the website for additional information.

511 10th St., N.W. • tel 202-347-4833 • nps.gov/foth or fords.org • Metro: Metro Center, Gallery Place–Chinatown, Archives–Navy Memorial–Penn Quarter

IN **THE KNOW**

Only a few vestiges remain of Washington's original Chinese neighborhood; most of it has long been subsumed by Penn Quarter, with small remnants found in Chinese-written street signs, the colorful **Friendship Arch** on H Street, and the annual Chinese New Year Parade. If you find yourself craving Chinese cuisine among the wide selection of ethnic cuisines on offer here, dig your chopsticks into some chow foon at **China Boy** (817 6th St., N.W.) or **Chinatown Express** (746 6th St., N.W.).

Smithsonian American Art Museum and National Portrait Gallery

5 In this noble Greek Revival space modeled on the Pantheon, you'll find the nation's oldest federal American art collection, spanning more than three centuries. Part of the building also houses the National Portrait Gallery, celebrating national heroes, intellects, rogues, and presidents. On the first floor, the "**Experience America**" exhibit showcases paintings created in 1934 as part of the pilot program to put artists to work. After you climb the grand staircase to the second floor, turn to the right for portraits of the U.S. presidents; to the left is the Smithsonian American Art Museum. You can begin in either direction, but this itinerary suggests going left first.

The American paintings are arranged in chronological order, kicking off with Early America and proceeding through Western Art, Landscapes, the Civil War, Impressionism, the Gilded Age, and Modernism. Seek out Catlin's Native Americans; Albert Bierstadt's celebratory Western landscapes, including the striking "Among the Sierra Nevada, California"; and John La Farge's stained-glass windows, "Peacocks & Peonies I and II."

Afterward, backtrack (or walk through the temporary exhibits at the end of the corridor, beyond "Modernism") to the start of the "America's Presidents" exhibit, all arranged in chronological order. These aren't necessarily the official White House portraits; some are staged, others are more fun. Highlights include Gilbert Stuart's famous "Lansdowne" portrait of George Washington; George P. A. Healy's pensive Abraham Lincoln; and Grover Cleveland's portrait in French Impressionist style,

DOWNTOWN

Life masks of Abraham Lincoln from 1860 (left) and 1865 (center) convey the toll of the Civil War.

to which the President proclaimed: "As for my ugly mug, I think the artist has 'struck it off' in great shape." Bill Clinton's portrait by Chuck Close is a series of abstract modules all working together to give him a digital look. Good explanations accompany all.

The grand staircase leads to yet another floor with more exhibits. Take note of the gorgeous **Great Hall** itself, once America's largest room. Conceived in the American Victorian Renaissance style to hold the mini-models required by inventors when the building housed the U.S. Patent Office, it's a glorious celebration of bygone days.

800 G St., N.W. ; enter via F St., N.W. • tel 202-633-1000 • americanart.si.edu, npg.si.edu • Metro: Gallery Place–Chinatown

International Spy Museum

6 Upon entering this fun, interactive museum, you pick a secret identity and are immediately swept up into the shadowy world of espionage. Your task: As you make your way through the various state-of-the-art exhibits, you must maintain your cover. Do you have what it takes to be a spy? Find out as you learn about a spy's motives (politics, patriotism, money) and the skills, training, and expertise required for success. Real agents and spy catchers such as CIA masters of disguise helped design the museum, with exhibits incorporating more than 600 real-life objects, including popular G-man toys from the 1930s and '40s ("G" for "government"), a KGB lipstick gun, and radio transmitters disguised as nails. Next are a series of themed rooms full of historic tales and artifacts related to such spymasters as Harriet Tubman, Elizabeth I, George Washington, and Julia Child. Downstairs, walk through the life and times of über-glamour-spy James Bond, a multiroom exhibition filled with artifacts and interactive stations.

800 F St., N.W. • tel 202 393 7798 • spymuseum.org • $$$$$; reserve tickets in advance to avoid long lines • Metro: Gallery Place–Chinatown

National Building Museum

7 This monumental, redbrick 1887 building, modeled after Rome's 16th-century Palazzo Farnese for the U.S. Pension Bureau headquarters, is now a fascinating museum devoted to architecture, urban planning, and design. In the airy **Great Hall**—as large as an American football field—enormous Corinthian columns tower 75 feet (23 m). The Great Hall's first two levels offer innovative changing exhibits; permanent collections include an exploration of what it means to live at home in America. Several rooms allow hands-on building for kids.

401 F St., N.W. • tel 202-272-2448 • nbm.org • closed Mon. • exhibitions: $$
• Metro: Judiciary Square, Gallery Place–Chinatown

Woolly Mammoth Theatre

8 After dinner at one of Penn Quarter's many buzzing restaurants, head to the theater. Edgy and outside-the-box Woolly Mammoth produces quirky, fun, original works that you would be hard-pressed to find anywhere else. Or try the acclaimed **Shakespeare Theatre Company at the Harman Center for the Arts** in two Penn Quarter locations (*Sidney Harman Hall, 610 F St., N.W., and Lansburgh Theatre, 450 7th St., N.W., tel 202-547-1122, shakespearetheatre.org*). Or catch a game or concert at the 20,000-seat **Verizon Center** (*601 F St., N.W., tel 202-628-3200, verizoncenter.monumentalnetwork.com*).

641 D St., N.W. • tel 202-393-3939 • woollymammoth.net
• Metro: Archives–Navy Memorial–Penn Quarter, Gallery Place–Chinatown

GOOD **EATS**

■ **JALEO**
Tapas in a festive setting, with good vegetarian options. **480 7th St., N.W., tel 202-628-7949, $$**

■ **CLYDE'S OF GALLERY PLACE**
Classic American dishes with a buzzing ambiance. **707 7th St., N.W., tel 202-349-3700, $$**

■ **NOPA KITCHEN + BAR**
An American-style brasserie famous for its twice-fried chicken. **800 F St., N.W., tel 202-347-1667, $–$$$**

Newseum

One of Washington's most interesting museums takes a look at news reporting around the world, both past and present.

Iconic images of heroism and horror form a special gallery of Pulitzer Prize winners.

The Newseum is exactly what its name implies: a museum and sanctuary for all things news. The building's transparent facade itself features a 74-foot-high (23 m) marble engraving of the First Amendment. Inside, seven levels of high-tech exhibits explore all aspects of the press. You could spend days absorbing the 15 fascinating permanent galleries and 15 state-of-the-art theaters. But for those short on time, or who might find it all a little overwhelming, here's a streamlined tour showcasing some highlights.

■ TODAY'S FRONT PAGES

Before entering the museum, peruse the day's front pages from all over the world displayed behind glass out front. It's interesting to note what each deems most important—local politics, sports, international crisis, or weather events.

■ CONCOURSE LEVEL

Begin with the four-minute overview film in the **Hearst Orientation Theaters,** which helps you understand the museum layout and formulate a game plan. On this level, too, you'll find the **Berlin Wall Gallery,** featuring eight 12-foot-high (4 m) concrete sections of the original wall, graffiti and all—the largest display outside Germany. Then take the elevator to the sixth level and work your way back down.

■ LEVEL SIX

Even those with the tightest schedule should step out onto the **Greenspun Terrace** to take in the panoramic views of the Capitol and National Mall. Note the **Pennsylvania Avenue Timeline** running the length of the terrace, giving a historical account of the famous street six floors below you.

■ LEVEL FIVE

The huge **News Corporation News History Gallery**—the museum's

SAVVY **TRAVELER**

The Newseum's exhibit showcasing today's front pages is a fascinating way to get the world's take on news—what's important to whom. For those who can't visit the Newseum every day, you can visit the website for the same info from the comfort of your own home: *newseum.org/todaysfrontpages.*

largest permanent gallery—is perhaps its most interesting exhibit as well. Front pages essentially summarizing 500 years of world history are displayed in easy-to-pull-out drawers, with insightful taglines providing context. Look for the front page of the *London Gazette* decrying the Great Fire of London in 1666; the *Massachusetts Gazette* announcing a tax revolt in the Colonies in 1765; Jesse James's assassination in Missouri's *Neosho Times* in 1882; and more, more, more. Next, duck into the five 25-seat theaters that explore issues that have confronted journalists through the ages. Also on this level, the **Smith Big Screen Theater** presents documentaries, historic news broadcasts, and breaking news on a 100-foot-long (30 m) video wall, with multiple images simultaneously projected. If breaking news happens, news feeds from around the globe will be tapped and presented right here.

■ LEVEL FOUR

Try to catch up with your kids in the social media realm by dabbling with various interactive experiences in the **New Media Gallery.** The museum's most sobering exhibit is nearby, the **9/11 Gallery,** where part of the wreckage of the World Trade Center's North Tower's broadcast tower, mangled and burned, is displayed. Placards and videos discuss the journalists' role in getting the news out on September 11, 2001, and a wall of relevant newspaper front pages from around the world hangs on one side.

■ LEVEL THREE

An enormous world map in the **Time Warner World News Gallery** provides an overview of the different levels of press freedom climate: Norway and Sweden are the most open, North Korea the most closed. The dangers journalists face—including kidnapping, torture, and murder—are also explored. Next, reflect on how radio, TV, and the Internet have revolutionized the news in the **Bloomberg Internet, TV and Radio Gallery,** where two large media walls feature famous broadcast events. And if you've timed your visit right, the **Knight Studio,** a state-of-the-art TV broadcast studio, may be on the air—you never know who might walk in! In the past the studio has hosted segments of *Good Morning America* and an NBC interview with President Barack Obama.

■ LEVEL TWO

If wandering the exhibits makes you want to try your hand at reporting, the **NBC News Interactive Newsroom** allows you to take your place in front of the camera and deliver a story from a teleprompter. Here, too, you can learn how to prepare a front-page story on individual touch-screen stations; test your investigative reporting skills to help solve a mysterious animal breakout at the zoo; and see how to capture the most compelling photograph of a river rescue.

IN **THE KNOW**

Glass and steel define the Newseum's state-of-the-art facade, designed by Polshek Partnership Architects. And symbolism abounds. The glass facade represents the openness of democracy, a "window on the world" looking out on Pennsylvania Avenue (and passersby can look in on the giant news screens). The facade's roof-to-sidewalk marble plaque showcases the first 45 words of the First Amendment—both summing up the museum's mission and fusing its ultra-contemporary design with the classical revival style of its neighboring buildings.

DOWNTOWN

LEVEL ONE

The remarkable **Pulitzer Prize Photographs Gallery** presents the most comprehensive collection of star photographs ever put on show. Many will look familiar: You'll see the U.S. Marines raising the flag at Iwo Jima (1945), Coretta Scott King consoling her daughter during Martin Luther King, Jr.'s funeral (1969), JFK and Dwight D. Eisenhower meeting at Camp David after the Bay of Pigs debacle (1961), Jack Ruby shooting Lee Harvey Oswald (1963), and many more images displaying some of the harshest as well as the most poignant times in world history. Visitors are also treated to interviews with the journalists behind the camera, revealing never-before-told stories.

Finally, enjoy **"I-Witness!"** at the Annenberg Theater, a 4-D movie (3-D plus seat movement and other physical special effects) that seemingly

Video of the dismantling and a portion of the Berlin Wall put you on the front line of the Cold War.

takes you to the scene where great reporters are doing their job, such as Nellie Bly going undercover in a 19th-century insane asylum and Edward R. Murrow on a London rooftop during World War II.

DOWNTOWN

555 Pennsylvania Ave., N.W. • tel 202-292-6100 • newseum.org • $$$$$ (ticket valid for two days)
• Metro: Archives–Navy Memorial–Penn Quarter, Judiciary Square

Theater Scene

Theatrical antics may prevail on Capitol Hill, but that shouldn't take away from the fact that Washington boasts one of the country's most thriving theater scenes, especially when it comes to experiential theater. Indeed, the numbers speak for themselves: 80-plus professional area theaters, more than 350 productions that run for more than 8,000 performances, more than 2 million audience members. When all is said and done, Washington is second only to New York in terms of the number of theater seats. And it's growing every year.

Above: President John F. Kennedy and First Lady Jacqueline exit the National Theater following the premiere of "Mr. President," on September 25, 1962. Opposite: "The Sisters Rosensweig," by Wendy Wasserstein, at Theater J, one of the District's many stages

In the Beginning

The ornate **National Theater**—called the "Theater of Presidents" for its proximity to the White House—opened its doors in 1835 (in a different building on the same spot), making it the country's third-oldest theater. **Ford's Theatre** opened in 1862 as Ford's Athenaeum and presented a mix of comedies, variety shows, and Shakespearean plays. Alas, it's most famous for being the venue of President Abraham Lincoln's assassination. Dozens of theaters lit up downtown D.C. in the early 20th century, with "polite" or "high-class" vaudeville for middle class audiences. These included the **Warner Theatre,** originally opened as the Earle Theatre in 1924; today it's a major host of Broadway shows, dance, film, and music concerts.

Regional Theater

Founded in 1950, **Arena Stage** was one of the nation's first not-for-profit theaters, dedicated to focusing on the "canvas of American theater," including classics and new works. Washington boasts several other lauded regional theaters, including the **Shakespeare Theatre Company,** and the **Signature Theatre** in Arlington, Virginia.

Neighborhood Revival

Washington's theater scene changed dramatically about 20 years ago, when the D.C. government smartly offered grants to convert empty buildings in struggling neighborhoods into artistic venues. Directors and producers jumped at the chance. Thus was born a whole slew of new small theaters, where experimental and risky tactics are tried out and innovation is favored—Woolly Mammoth, Studio Theatre, and Theater J among them. See what's on stage via *dctheatrescene.com*; discounted tickets are available at *Ticketplace.org* and *Goldstar.com*.

SMALL **THEATERS**

Regional theaters currently pushing the envelope include:

Atlas Performing Arts Center, 1333 H St., N.E., tel 202-399-7993, *atlasarts.org*

Signature Theatre, 4200 Campbell Ave., Arlington, VA, tel 703-820-9771, *sigtheatre.org*

Source, 1835 14th St., N.W., tel 202-204-7800, *culturaldc.org*

Studio Theatre, 1501 14th St., N.W., tel 202- 332-3300, *studiotheatre.org*

Theater J, 1529 16th St., N.W., tel 202-777-3210, *washingtondcjcc.org*

Woolly Mammoth Theatre Company, 641 D St., N.W., 202-393-3939, *woollymammoth.net*

DOWNTOWN

Small Museums

The National Mall's world-class museums may get all the attention, but Washington contains plenty of smaller museums that deserve a nod as well. The world's foremost museum devoted to women artists, a German brewer's Gilded Age manse, and a presidential summer cottage are among these hidden gems.

DOWNTOWN

■ NATIONAL MUSEUM
OF WOMEN IN THE ARTS
Showcasing more than 4,500 paintings and sculptures by more than 1,000 women artists, with work spanning from the 16th century to modern day, this lovely little museum founded in 1987 counts among its holdings stunning artwork by Frida Kahlo, Mary Cassatt, and Georgia O'Keeffe—indeed, it's considered the world's foremost collection of women's art. But it also celebrates talented women who didn't necessarily claim the fame they deserved. For examples, look for Lavinia Fontana's "Portrait of a Noblewoman" (ca 1580), Rosa Bonheur's "Highland Raid" (1860), and Justine Kurland's "Waterfall Mama Babies" (2006). The museum occupies a former Masonic Temple, built in glorious Renaissance Revival style.

1250 New York Ave., N.W.• tel 202-783-5000
• nmwa.org • $$ • Metro: Metro Center

■ NATIONAL POSTAL MUSEUM
Part of the Smithsonian Institution, the National Postal Museum is elegantly housed in the former Washington City Post Office, close by Union Station and designed by Graham and Burnham in 1914. The galleries, complete with interactive displays, explore topics such as the history of mail delivery, the passion of stamp collecting, the role of direct marketing, and the art of personal correspondence. A prop plane and a railway car are among the vintage modes of mail delivery on display in the 90-foot-high (27 m) atrium.

2 Massachusetts Ave., N.E. • tel 202-633-5555
• postalmuseum.si.edu • Metro: Union Station

■ CHARLES SUMNER SCHOOL
MUSEUM AND ARCHIVES
One of three historic public elementary schools for African-American children, and one of the District's few remaining

Classical and contemporary artists alike are represented in airy galleries within the National Museum of Women in the Arts.

landmarks devoted to early black history, the Charles Sumner School occupies a stately redbrick building erected in 1872. It's named for U.S. Senator Charles Sumner, a Massachusetts abolitionist who fervently fought for civil rights, including abolishing slavery in D.C. Slated for demolition in 1978, the building was saved by an organized community effort and today its museum and archives document the history of D.C.'s public schools.

17th & M Sts., N.W. • tel 202-661-7581
• culturaltourismdc.org • closed Sat.–Sun.
• Metro: Farragut North, Farragut West

■ HEURICH HOUSE MUSEUM
Washingtonians walk by this Romanesque Revival castle like home never realizing they can view what's inside: the ornate abode of turn-of-the-20th-century German brewer Christian Heurich, one of the foremost brewers in local history. Heurich arrived in the United States a poor immigrant in 1866 and, having learned the brewing trade from his father, started a brewery. In time, Christian Heurich Brewing Company became Washington's second largest employer, after the federal government. When Heurich had this

house built (between 1892 and 1894), it was one of the city's first Gilded Age mansions. After his death, Heurich's descendants deeded the house to what became the Historical Society of Washington. A self-guided tour takes you through 11 rooms on three levels. Lavish decorations include a marble mosaic floor in the main hall, a Tiffany chandelier, and elaborately carved furniture in the dining room. Don't miss the beautiful Victorian garden.

1307 New Hampshire Ave., N.W.
• tel 202-429-1894 • heurichhouse.org
• closed Sun.–Wed.; call ahead for tour reservations • $ • Metro: Dupont Circle

■ KREEGER MUSEUM

Tucked away on 5.5 sculpture-dotted acres (2.2 ha) in the wooded Foxhall neighborhood of Northwest D.C., this private art museum showcases Impressionists and American artists from the 1850s to the 1970s, collected by insurance executive David Lloyd

The Catherine the Great Easter Egg, crafted by Fabergé, at the Hillwood Museum

DOWNTOWN

Kreeger and his wife, Carmen. Nine paintings by Claude Monet, a graceful Alexander Calder mobile hanging in the grand staircase, and a series of Picassos (the Kreegers' favorite artist) that trace his career are just a few of the highlights. The impressive collection also includes traditional art from Africa and Asia. The house alone is worth the visit—it's one of just a few examples in Washington, D.C., of work by postmodernist architect Philip Johnson. Classical and jazz concerts are sometimes offered after hours.

2401 Foxhall Road, N.W. • tel 202-337-3050 • kreegermuseum.org • Tues.–Thurs. by reservation only (tel 202-338-3552 or email visitorservices@kreegermuseum.org), Fri.–Sat. no reservation needed; closed Sun.–Mon. • $$ • Not Metro accessible

■ HILLWOOD ESTATE, MUSEUM, AND GARDENS

During her lifetime, cereal heiress Marjorie Merriweather Post furnished her 36-room neo-Georgian mansion with her exquisite and extensive collection of imperial Russian and 18th- and 19th-century French decorative arts with the idea that someday it would become a museum. That day came in 1977. Hillwood is a rare peek into the lavish home of a 20th-century socialite, filled with such treasures as Russian icons, Fabergé eggs, and

French tapestries. The house itself is stunning, with its formal Louis XVI drawing room, private movie theater, and ballroom. Equally impressive are the extensive gardens bordering Rock Creek Park, 25 acres (10 ha) of lush lawns, formal gardens, and peaceful woodlands. Special areas include a Japanese-style garden with a cascading waterfall and a lovely French parterre with a fountain.

4155 Linnean Ave., N.W. • tel 202-686-5807 • hillwoodmuseum.org • closed Mon., some Sun., and most of Jan. • $$$ • Metro: Van Ness–UDC

■ PRESIDENT LINCOLN'S COTTAGE

The 16th president spent summers during the Civil War at this 34-room Gothic Revival "cottage" about 3 miles (5 km) north of the White House's bustle, on the grounds of the Old Soldiers' Home. Here, surrounded by open green countryside, on one of the city's highest points, Lincoln could relax in the breeze—though it wasn't all fun and games. He orchestrated much of his Civil War business from here, including drafting the Emancipation Proclamation. Guided tours take you through the period-decorated rooms, telling tales of daily life.

140 Rock Creek Church Rd., N.W. • tel 202-829-0436 • lincolncottage.org • $$$ • Metro: Georgia Avenue–Petworth

White House & Around

In 1/91, architect and civil planner Pierre-Charles L'Enfant, under the direction of President George Washington, chose the site for the President's House—on a hill at one end of the city, about a mile from the future U.S. Capitol.

Irish-born architect James Hoban drew the winning design, based on the Duke of Leicester's palace near Dublin. As the house was not ready for residents until 1800, John Adams was the first president to move in. The neighborhood grew in tandem, becoming a focus of political power and attracting such governmental edifices as the Eisenhower Executive Office Building and the Department of the Treasury, as well as the charming 18th-century town houses edging Lafayette Park. Today, intermingling with the official, are more approachable churches, luxury hotels, and art museums.

◐ The aptly named Red Room of the White House, of late used as a reception room and to host small dinner gatherings with the president

WHITE HOUSE & AROUND

White House & Around

The People's House is the centerpiece of this stroll through Washington's historic heart.

4 Decatur House (see pp. 111–112)
Learn about the life and times of the hero of the War of 1812, and those who came after him, in this beautifully curated historic house on Lafayette Square. Walk north on 17th St., N.W.

5 National Geographic Society (see p. 112)
Exciting interactive exhibits delve into the successes of this foremost research and exploration institution. Backtrack down 17th St., N.W., cutting across Farragut Square to the corner of Pennsylvania Ave., N.W.

3 St. John's Episcopal Church (see pp. 111)
Find the pew reserved for presidents before crossing H St., N.W., and walking one block west.

6 Renwick Gallery (see pp. 112–113)
You'll be wowed by this newly renovated museum's dedication to the future of art. Cross Pennsylvania Ave., N.W., and proceed south on 17th St., N.W., bearing right on New York Ave., N.W.

7 Octagon House (see p. 114)
This oddly shaped historic house has served more than once as the president's house. Proceed south on 18th St., N.W.

8 Art Museum of the Americas & Organization of American States (see pp. 114–115) Enjoy the small art gallery and relax in the secret indoor tropical garden—especially beloved in winter. Backtrack on 17th St., N.W., turning into the President's Park at State Pl., N.W.

9 The Ellipse (see p. 116–117)
Stroll across this grassy expanse, site of the nation's Christmas tree, along with a fabulous view of the back of the White House. Continue across the Ellipse, making your way to 15th St., N.W., at Pennsylvania Ave., N.W.

10 Willard InterContinental (see p. 117) The legendary hotel is a great place to end your walk with a refreshing drink.

2 Lafayette Square (see p. 110) Admire stately statues, relax on a shady bench, and get a different perspective on the White House from this lovely park. Then stroll to the square's north side.

1 White House (see pp. 118–121) Lucky you if you have tickets to visit the White House. If not, stop by the White House Visitor Center. Then head to Lafayette Square, just north of the White House across pedestrianized Pennsylvania Avenue.

0 100 meters
0 100 yards

Hotel

H STREET

St. John's Episcopal Church

Decatur House

Lafayette Square 2

Renwick Gallery

Eisenhower Executive Office Building

MADISON PL.

PENNSYLVANIA AVE.

(no public access)

(closed to vehicles)

White House 1

PRESIDENT'S PARK

Zero Milestone

Sherman Statue

National Christmas Tree Site

Ellipse Visitor Pavillion

(no public access)

STATE PL.

G ST.

F ST.

E STREET

17TH ST.

Octagon House 7

American National Red Cross

Organization of American States 8

Art Museum of the Americas

NEW YORK AVE.

18TH ST.

C ST N.W.

C STREET

E STREET

15TH ST.

14TH STREET

PENN. AVE. N.

PENN. AVE. S.

PERSHING PARK

White House Visitor Center

Willard Inter-Continental 10

12TH STREET

WHITE HOUSE & AROUND   DISTANCE: 3.25 MILES (5.2 KM)   TIME: APPROX. 6 HOURS   METRO: FARRAGUT WEST, FARRAGUT NORTH, METRO CENTER

WHITE HOUSE & AROUND

The Jacqueline Kennedy Garden flourishes outside the White House's east wing.

White House

1 See pp. 118–121.

White House: 1600 Pennsylvania Ave., N.W.; White House Visitor Center: 1450 Pennsylvania Ave., N.W. • tel 202-456-7041 • whitehouse.gov, nps.gov/whho • public tour requests must be submitted through your member of Congress three weeks to six months ahead of your visit • Metro: Federal Triangle, Metro Center, McPherson Square

Lafayette Square

2 This graceful, tree-shaded park facing the White House —with plenty of benches to rest your feet—has seen its share of demonstrations for or against something: nuclear disarmament, peace in Tibet, women's right to vote, or whatever is the political discord of the day. Part of the "President's Park" (though it lost the physical connection when Pennsylvania Avenue was cut through in 1804), the square centers on Clark Mills's **"Major Gen. Andrew Jackson"** on a rearing horse, the first cast-bronze equestrian statue made in the United States. On the park's four corners, statues of foreign-born Revolutionary War heroes include France's **"Marquis de Lafayette"** (southeast corner) and **"Comte de Rochambeau"** (southwest); Prussia's **"Baron Friedrich Wilhelm von Steuben"** (northwest); and Poland's **"Gen. Thaddeus Kosciuszko"** (northeast). Many of the fashionable 18th-century houses edging the square once housed Washington's elite; saved from the wrecking ball by a determined Jacqueline Kennedy, many today serve as White House offices.

North of the White House, H St. bet. 15th & 17th Sts., N.W. • tel 202-208-1631 • nps.gov/whho • Metro: McPherson Square, Farragut West

WHITE HOUSE & AROUND

St. John's Episcopal Church

3 This little yellow stucco church across from the White House has hosted every president since James Madison for at least a bit of time—hence its nickname, Church of the Presidents. James Madison's wife, Dolley, was baptized and confirmed here, and Franklin Delano Roosevelt prayed here on both of his inauguration days. Designed by famed architect Benjamin Henry Latrobe (who helped design both the White House and Capitol), it opened its doors in 1816. Check out **Pew No. 54,** the President's Pew, reserved for the president should he or she decide to attend. Paul Revere's son Joseph cast the 1,000-pound (454 kg) bell in the steeple in 1822.

1525 H St., N.W. • tel 202-347-8766 • stjohns-dc.org • Metro: Farragut North, Farragut West, McPherson Square

GOOD **EATS**

■ **BREADLINE**
Yummy, healthy salads, soups, and sandwiches.
1751 Pennsylvania Ave., N.W., tel 202-822-8900, $

■ **FOUNDING FARMERS**
Eco-chic American cuisine using local ingredients.
1924 Pennsylvania Ave., N.W., tel 202-822-8783, $$–$$$

■ **TEAISM**
Asian-inspired light fare.
800 Connecticut Ave., N.W., tel 202-835-2233, $$

Decatur House

4 New energy is being brought into this historic home on Lafayette Square, with enthralling stories about life in the early capital throughout the free guided tour. This three-story federal-style house was originally built for Commodore Stephen Decatur, Jr., naval hero of the War of 1812. Designed by famed architect Benjamin Henry Latrobe, it was completed in 1818—but Decatur barely had the chance to enjoy the place. He was killed in a duel with a fellow officer 14 months after moving in. His wife rented the house to the likes of Henry Clay and Martin Van Buren. Today visitors are taken across the elegant brick courtyard into various rooms, including the parlor rooms and the ballroom, much of which emanate with the aura of a later owner, Mrs. Truxtun Beale, who presided over a salon for ambassadors and politicians. The tour ends in Washington's only extant slave quarters. If your schedule doesn't permit joining a tour, check the website for the interesting special exhibitions that take place in the parlor rooms. On Thursday evenings May through September, jazz musicians play under the stars in the beautiful courtyard; reserve tickets in advance.

Enter at 1610 H St., N.W. • tel 202-218-4300 • whitehousehistory.org • tours Mon., Wed., & Fri. (Mon. only in winter), 11 a.m., 12:30 p.m., & 2 p.m.; check website for special exhibitions • Metro: Farragut North, Farragut West, McPherson Square

National Geographic Society

5 Established in 1888 to support the exploration of the world's farthest reaches, this revered institution has sponsored such big-name explorers as Jacques Cousteau, Jane Goodall, and Sylvia Earle. The main headquarters comprises the three buildings clustered here, home to the Society's flagship "yellow-bordered" magazine, as well as the National Geographic Channel, *National Geographic Traveler* magazine, National Geographic Travel Books, classroom materials—and the list goes on. As you enter through the 17th Street entrance, look up to the ceiling between the elevators at the marvelous 3-D relief of the **Grand Canyon.** Then delve into the two temporary exhibits presented at **Explorers Hall;** they're tied into recent NatGeo activities, with examples of previous exhibits including geckos, da Vinci's inventions, and Xi'an's terra-cotta warriors. There's always a free photography exhibit presented "beneath the stars" in the building across the courtyard (the stars represent how the night sky looked when the Society was founded in 1888). A lively lecture series, lunchtime films, and other events are available as well; check the website. If it's lunchtime, you can dine at the staff cafeteria, or grab a coffee or snack at the snack bar.

1145 17th St., N.W. • tel 202-857-7000 • nationalgeographic.com • $$$ • Metro: Farragut North, Farragut West

Renwick Gallery

6 The architecturally distinctive Renwick Gallery, dating from 1859, was the first public building in America designed specifically to showcase works of art to the public. Along these lines, the

Smithsonian American Art Museum used the building to display its contemporary craft program between 1972 and 2013. After an extensive two-year renovation a whole new chapter began when the museum reopened with a brand-new focus looking toward art in the 21st century and American genius. Mind-boggling exhibitions are the goal—the inaugural exhibit, for example, was called "Wonder" and focused on gallery-size installations including one room with walls full of intricate, spiraling, wallpaper-like designs—all made from dead bugs; green marbles flowing across a floor and up the walls to represent the Chesapeake; and the mold of a hemlock tree hollowed out and hand-carved to resemble the original tree. It's a magnificent look into the future of art.

1661 Pennsylvania Ave., N.W. • tel 202-633-7970 • renwick.americanart.si.edu • Metro: Farragut West, Farragut North

The Renwick Gallery hosts innovative American art such as Patrick Dougherty's "Shindig."

Octagon House

7 Standing bravely in the shadow of austere modern edifices, the Octagon House was built about the same time as the White House for a prominent Virginia planter, John Tayloe III, and his wife, Ann Ogle Tayloe. Designed by the first architect of the Capitol, Dr. William Thornton, and completed by 1801, it was the neighborhood's first private residence at a time when little else existed in the area. Its true claim to fame, however, is the role it served as the residence of James and Dolley Madison after the British burned the nearby President's House in 1814. Just a few months later, in February 1815, Madison signed the war-ending Treaty of Ghent in an upstairs parlor. Bought by the American Institute of Architects in 1902, it has been extensively renovated back to its Tayloe-era look. Take a self-guided tour through the sparsely decorated rooms—including the drawing room, dining room, upstairs parlors, Treaty Room/Study, and basement.

1799 New York Ave., N.W. • tel 202-626-7439 • architectsfoundation.org/preservation • open Thurs.–Sat. • Metro: Farragut West, Farragut North

Art Museum of the Americas & Organization of American States

8 The Organization of American States has two parts—an art museum, entered via 18th St., N.W., and the actual OAS building, entered around the block via 17th St., N.W. Begin with the small Art Museum of the Americas, showcasing rotating pieces from its permanent collection; traveling shows of Latin America and Caribbean art and photography take place as well. Don't miss the blue-tiled loggia, adorned in Aztec and Inca designs.

Exiting, backtrack half a block to C St., N.W., turn right to 17th St., N.W., and right again, to the grandiose facade of the Organization of American States headquarters. The OAS is a regional alliance of 35 member countries from the Americas and the Caribbean promoting peace and economic cooperation among its members. Admire the building's striking mix of classical and

Spanish Colonial architecture, proclaimed an architectural wonder when it opened in 1910. A statue of **"Queen Isabella the Catholic"** greets you in front, a reminder that Spain sponsored Christopher Columbus's travel that led to the European discovery of America. Walk up the stairs and enter the building. You'll have to go through security and leave a piece of identification in exchange for a badge, but then you can roam as you please. Right away you'll come to the lovely **tropical**

An inner courtyard conveys the lush tropical home environments of members of the Organization of American States.

garden patio, an oasis of rubber, fig, coffee, and banana plants centered on a pink marble fountain. President William Howard Taft planted the **Peace Tree,** a hybrid of fig and rubber, during the building's dedication ceremonies. Behind the garden, a hall hosts changing exhibits related to the Americas and the Caribbean. Climb the massive staircase to the second floor, where the **Hall of Flags and Heroes** greets you with flags of all OAS members, as well as busts of national heroes—including George Washington, Simón Bolívar, and José de San Martín. Finally, step into the adjacent, elegant **Hall of the Americas,** where the Panama Canal Treaties were signed in 1977.

Art Museum of the Americas: 201 18th St., N.W., Organization of American States headquarters: 200 17th St., N.W.• tel 202-370-5000 • oas.org • Metro: Farragut West

IN **THE KNOW**

The first Christmas tree gracing the Ellipse dates to 1923, when President Calvin Coolidge "pushed the button" to light a 48-foot (14.6 m) balsam fir from his home state of Vermont. Various trees were either lit elsewhere on the grounds or live ones were trucked in from other states until 1978, when a Colorado spruce from Pennsylvania was planted on the spot. (At the time of writing, the current tree is a Colorado spruce from Virginia.)

Every president continues the traditional rite of lighting the National Christmas Tree each year following a festive musical extravaganza. Smaller trees representing the fifty states, the District of Columbia, and U.S. territories, flank the bigger tree along the "Pathway of Peace," and model trains chug around in one of the city's most festive settings.
thenationaltree.org

Each year the large National Christmas Tree, ceremoniously lit by the president, is visited by some 400,000 people.

The Ellipse

On the White House's south side, the Ellipse is a 52-acre (21 ha) grassy area surrounded by an oval drive. Entering from 17th Street, N.W., at State Place, N.W., stroll up the walk to the iron fence guarding the South Lawn. From here, you get fabulous views of the back of the **White House.** The **Truman Balcony** was controversial when President Truman proposed it in 1947—the president arguing it was a needed solution to provide shade for the family, the purists stating such an atrocity would destroy the federal look of the exterior. Truman, of course, won, and today it's a lovely place for the first family to relax and entertain—and enjoy some of the house's best views out onto the Mall. The expanse of grass and garden flanking the White House, the **South Lawn** is where formal and informal ceremonies take place, including the Easter Egg Roll every spring. If you're lucky, you might spy a military helicopter—Marine One—buzzing overhead, bringing the president home. Tucked away among the foliage are a jogging track, a swimming pool, a basketball court, and a tennis court. If you turn around and face the other way, you'll see the **National Christmas Tree** that's decorated every holiday season, a tradition that began with

President Calvin Coolidge in 1923 (see sidebar opposite). Here, too, is the 4-foot-high (1.2 m) **Zero Milestone,** where all road distances in the United States were to originate. That never happened; instead, only roads in Washington, D.C., are measured from here. It's the best place to take a photo of the White House.

Just south of the White House • tel 202-208-1631 • nps.gov • Metro: Farragut West, Metro Center

Willard InterContinental

The story goes that the term "lobbyist" was first used at this grand, beaux arts–style hotel, when those seeking favors or inside information cornered presidents and politicians in the lobby. The truth is that the word was used long before, in reference to the House of Commons, but there's no doubt the Willard's importance as a meeting place invigorated the use of the term in the Capital City. Charles Dickens, Nathaniel Hawthorne, Harry Houdini, Mae West, and countless presidents, foreign dignitaries, literati, and glitterati have all been honored guests. During the Civil War, Julia Ward Howe wrote "The Battle Hymn of the Republic" in her room here; more than a hundred years later, Martin Luther King, Jr., added the finishing touches to his "I Have a Dream" speech while in the Willard's lobby. Established in the 1850s and rebuilt from the ground up in its current style in 1904, the hotel closed in mid-1968 after racial rioting following the assassination of Martin Luther King, Jr.; Congress saved it from demolition by designating it as a historic landmark. It reopened in all of its previous opulence in 1986. With three restaurants, the famed **Round Robin Bar** (likely the oldest operating bar in D.C.), and its proximity to the White House, the Willard has become a monument unto itself. At the very least, go in and admire its lavish lobby. Or step it up a notch and enjoy afternoon tea at **Peacock Alley** to the strains of harp music.

1401 Pennsylvania Ave., N.W. • tel 202-628-9100 • ihg.com • Metro: Metro Center

White House

See the official residence and workplace of the president of the United States, filled with treasures from presidents past and present.

WHITE HOUSE & AROUND

Hannibal keeps watch over the White House Blue Room from a circa 1817 mantel clock.

Every U.S. president except George Washington has lived in this most famous of residences. The District of Columbia's oldest public building, its construction began in 1792 and was completed eight years later. In its 132 rooms, the president meets with national and foreign leaders, signs bills into law, hosts state dinners, briefs the press, all the while trying to lead a private family life. The only way for the general public to visit is by contacting your congressperson up to six months in advance to arrange a self-guided tour.

You will be sent a timed ticket ahead of your visit. Bring it at your appointed time to the south side of the East Executive Avenue entrance and go through a security check; you will eventually end up at the White House's ground level. Walk through the **East Colonnade,** adorned with historic photos of presidential life in the White House to the right; views onto the **South Lawn,** with the Washington Monument rising in the distance, are to the left. You then enter the ground floor of the White House.

■ LIBRARY

This pretty room was originally used as a laundry room, until President Theodore Roosevelt turned it into the servants' locker room in 1902. It became the official library in 1935, and ever since has held important tomes on American thought and tradition—2,700 to date. The room, tastefully decorated in late federal period style including furniture by New York cabinetmaker Duncan Phyfe, is often used for teas, press interviews, and small meetings.

■ EAST ROOM

Walk up the steps and enter the house's largest room, decorated in late 18th-century classical style. Here's where state dinners, receptions,

SAVVY **TRAVELER**

Even if you haven't been able to arrange a tour of the White House itself, the **White House Visitor Center** provides a fascinating introduction to life within the Executive Mansion. Interactive exhibits tell behind-the-scenes stories, including the usher's role, the evolution of the Oval Office, and surprising presidential menu requests (including Garfield's squirrel soup). Don't miss the video narrated by the president that adds personal notes of residents past and present of what it means to live in America's most famous residence.

dances, concerts, weddings, award presentations, press conferences, and bill-signing ceremonies take place. Union troops were quartered here during the Civil War, and this is where the bodies of Abraham Lincoln and John F. Kennedy were laid in state. First kids have taken a liking to its expanse as well—Tad Lincoln fashioned a sleigh out of a kitchen chair and two goats and took a ride across its Fontainebleau parquetry oak floor. Jimmy Carter's daughter, Amy, roller-skated here, leaving marks that weren't fixed for 30 years. And Abigail Adams hung her family's laundry in this unfinished room when she and John moved into the damp residence. Note the portrait of George Washington by

Gilbert Stuart—it's the same painting that Dolley Madison removed as the British descended to burn the White House in 1814, and thus it's the only piece in the White House that remains since its first occupancy in 1800.

■ GREEN ROOM

The first of three state parlors on the first floor, the Green Room has always been a popular place for small meetings and tea. Thomas Jefferson hosted dinners here, and here James Madison signed the nation's first declaration of war—the War of 1812. As part of her program to give the White House a more dignified, museum-like look, Jacqueline Kennedy selected its delicate green watered-silk fabric in 1962. Be sure to note the silver coffee urn, belonging to John and Abigail Adams; and the French candlesticks, owned by James and Dolley Madison.

■ BLUE ROOM

This elegant, elliptical-shaped room is the most formal of the parlor rooms, where the president officially receives kings and heads of state during receptions. James Monroe had the room decorated in the French Empire style in 1817—the seven gold chairs, the sofa, and the mantel clock date from that time. It was Martin Van Buren

who added the color blue, in 1837. Don't miss George P. A. Healy's 1859 portrait of John Tyler on the west wall, considered to be the finest in the series of presidential portraits. The principal White House Christmas tree sparkles in this room every year.

■ RED ROOM

The American Empire style popular in the early 1800s is striking in this opulently decorated room, though it's perhaps the vibrant red color—in the red twill satin fabric on the walls, as well as in the red-silk-and-gold-trimmed furniture—that hits you first. Theodore Roosevelt favored the Red Room as a smoking room, and today it continues to be used as an after-dinner parlor. The marble mantel has been in the White House since 1819.

■ STATE DINING ROOM

Designed in the style of neoclassical English houses of the late 18th century, the State Dining Room can host up to 140 guests at its mahogany dining table. When a state dinner is not in the works, the table is often adorned with James Madison's French Empire porcelain. George P. A. Healy's 1869 portrait of a contemplative Abraham Lincoln hanging over the fireplace was given to the White House by the family in 1939.

The red carpet is ready to be rolled out for high occasions along the Cross Hall, connecting the State Dining Room with the East Room of the White House.

■ CROSS HALL & ENTRANCE FOYER

At the end of the tour, visitors are guided through the glistening marble floors and walls of the Cross Hall, which connects the State Dining Room with the East Room. A gallery of recent presidential portraits hangs from the walls, and the stunning cut-glass chandeliers were made in London about 1775. Join the line to take a selfie beneath the Presidential Seal, and then you are given the honor of leaving through the **Entrance Foyer** and out the official front door.

White House: 1600 Pennsylvania Ave., N.W.; White House Visitor Center: 1450 Pennsylvania Ave., N.W. • tel 202-456-7041 • whitehouse.gov, nps.gov/whho • public tour requests must be submitted through your member of Congress three weeks to six months ahead of your visit • Metro: Federal Triangle, Metro Center, McPherson Square

Presidential Washington

As you tour Washington, D.C., reminders are everywhere that you're on P.O.T.U.S.'s turf—the White House at 1600 Pennsylvania Avenue, N.W., of course, is the most obvious giveaway. But chances are, you'll also experience blocked streets, motorcades, and the excitement of the Marine One helicopter whirring overhead. Washington has been the president's town since the beginning—whether you like it or not.

Inauguration day brings out crowds of visitors to launch the new leader of the United States, from the solemn swearing-in on the steps of the Capitol (Barack Obama, 2013, above) to exuberant parades down Pennsylvania Avenue (John F. Kennedy, 1961, opposite).

The President's House

The White House stands proudly behind iron gates, a draw for photo-snapping tourists from near and far. Through the years, the home and office of the president have become an enduring symbol of leadership and political freedom in America and around the world. The media's common attribution "according to the White House" shows how the physical house has become united with the ideals of the chief executive—and the nation that elected him or her—who resides within.

Inauguration Day

Every four years, Washington, D.C., decks itself out to welcome the new (or reelected) president, a tradition that began with George Washington in 1789, a week after he was inaugurated in New York City. The official swearing in takes place in front of the Capitol on the third Monday of January (a local holiday), with the entire Mall becoming packed with people who either watch with their naked eyes if they're close enough, or from the Jumbotrons positioned all along the Mall. Afterward, parties abound—there are several official inaugural balls, which you must *be* someone or *know* someone who's someone to get in. The president and first lady make a personal appearance at each one. But there are plenty of other parties for normal folk to attend too, sponsored by state societies, businesses, and private organizations.

Motorcades

The president always travels with his or her Secret Service motorcade—a long line of motorcycles, black SUVs, and police cars, all flashing lights and sirens for protection. Other dignitaries have motorcades too, of varying sizes; the car carrying a foreign dignitary will fly their national flag on the hood. You know it's the president motorcade because an ambulance always trails behind . . . just in case.

THE PRESIDENTS' RACE **BASEBALL STYLE**

Should you attend a home game with the Washington Nationals baseball team, you'll witness the "Presidents' Race" in the middle of the fourth inning—pitting up to six presidents (Washington, Jefferson, Lincoln, Theodore Roosevelt, Coolidge, and Taft) against one another in a foot race around the outfield. There are no rules, and the winner is not necessarily predetermined. Pick your prez and cheer him on!

Secret Statues

Washington is filled with statues extolling noteworthy people and events throughout history. Here are some of the more intriguing, less obvious ones.

■ EINSTEIN MEMORIAL

Looking like an overstuffed teddy bear, a rough-hewn, chunky, bronze sculpture of Albert Einstein by Robert Berks sits near the Mall on the grounds of the National Academy of Sciences, where the esteemed scientist became a member in 1942. The sculpture celebrates Einstein's three most important scientific contributions: the photoelectric effect, the theory of general relativity, and the equivalence of energy and matter. But perhaps the most endearing thing about this 12-foot (4 m) statue is that kids can climb up into his lap—an ingenious photo op!

National Academy of Sciences, 2101 Constitution Ave., N.W. • tel 202-334-2000 • Metro: Foggy Bottom–GWU

■ EMANCIPATION MEMORIAL

Dedicated on the 11th anniversary of Lincoln's assassination in 1876, the statue in Lincoln Park, on Capitol Hill, predates the more famous Lincoln statue on the National Mall. Here, a bronze President Lincoln stands proudly next to a kneeling, seemingly subservient former slave. Though heralded at the time of its creation, it has evolved into controversy; some feel the statue fails to show the role African-Americans—including black Union soldiers—played in fighting for their own emancipation.

Lincoln Park, East Capitol St., S.E., bet. 11th & 13th Sts. • tel 202-690-5185 • Metro: Stadium–Armory

■ TITANIC MEMORIAL

This cinematic granite statue of an angelic man seemingly sailing through the air, head raised and arms extended, commemorates the men who gave their lives when the famous ship sank in 1912 so that the women and children could live. Gertrude Vanderbilt Whitney, American sculptor, art patron, and founder of New York's Whitney Museum of Art, designed the statue in 1931.

Washington Channel Park, near 4th & P Sts., S.W., along Southwest Waterfront • Metro: Waterfront

A suitably larger-than-life statue of T. R. Roosevelt hails visitors to Roosevelt Island.

■ THEODORE ROOSEVELT ISLAND NATIONAL MEMORIAL

It will take a little doing to find the only statue in the nation's capital dedicated to the 26th president of the United States—but it's worth it. Head to Theodore Roosevelt Island in the Potomac River across from George-town. Surrounded by woods, the Great Conservationist no doubt would have loved his position here.

Northern tip of Theodore Roosevelt Island, accessible via the pedestrian footbridge just north of Roosevelt Bridge or via a walkway south of Key Bridge, both on the Virginia side of the Potomac River • tel 703-289-2500 • nps.gov/this • Metro: Rosslyn

■ ADAMS MEMORIAL

Sculptured by the renowned artist Augustus Saint-Gaudens, this haunting statue honors Clover Adams, wife of Henry Adams, who committed suicide in 1885. Adams commissioned the sculptor to create a memorial that would capture the Buddhist notion of Nirvana. It can be tough to find; look on a hillside in the cemetery's eastern end. Another option is to see a repro-duction in the Smithsonian American Art Museum (see pp. 93–94).

Rock Creek Cemetery, St. Paul's Episcopal Church, 201 Allison St., N.W. • tel 202-726-2080 • rockcreekparish.org • Metrobus: 60, H8

Dupont Circle & Beyond

Taking in an enticing mix of neighborhoods, this walk begins at Dupont Circle, centered around a lovely marble fountain. Back in the 1870s, the surrounding neighborhood, called Pacific Circle, drew society's crème de la crème—mining, steel, and shipping tycoons who held elaborate receptions and musicals in their beaux arts mansions. Today, simply strolling the streets and admiring these homes is a delight. You'll also find cafés, galleries, and small museums, notably the nationally acclaimed Phillips Collection. Nearby 14th Street is a hotbed of hip restaurants, bars, and boutiques. Just north, U Street takes on a more bohemian attitude, sprinkled with African-American landmarks. And north from here, Adams Morgan is a colorful Latino realm with more small shops, restaurants, and bars—with Ethiopian influences mingled in as well.

○   **Cyclists and pedestrians
    go about daily life near
    hopping U Street, N.W.**

Dupont Circle & Beyond

Start this walk through some of D.C.'s diverse Northwest neighborhoods a little later in the day, so you can take full advantage of the evening offerings.

❻ U Street, N.W. (see pp. 133–134) Bohemia meets ethnic diversity on this eclectic street alive with restaurants, clubs, and shops, plus some important African-American landmarks. Stay on U St, N.W., following it west to 18th St, N.W.

❼ Adams Morgan (see pp. 134–135) Explore bookshops, global cuisine, and coffee shops by day, hopping bars and salsa-imbued lounges by night in this favorite multicultural neighborhood.

KALORAMA

KALORAMA

WYOMING AVE.

WYOMING AVE.

ROAD

CONNECTICUT AV.

20TH STREET

19TH STREET

CALIFORNIA ST.

VERNON ST.

18TH STREET

COLUMBIA RD.

ADAMS MORGAN

Adams Morgan ❼

CHAMPLAIN ST.

ONTARIO RD.

17TH ST.

CRESCENT PL.

KALORAMA ROAD

FLORIDA AVE.

U STREET

V ST.

Meridian International Center

MERIDIAN HILL PARK

CARDOZO

V STREET

U STREET

U Street N.W. ❻

13TH ST.

Lincoln Theatre

Ben's Chili Bowl

U Street-African

0   200 meters
0   200 yards

① Dupont Circle
(see pp. 130–131)
A gracious fountain-centered circle in the heart of a residential neighborhood serves as a meeting place for all walks of life. Go up Connecticut Ave., N.W., to Q St., N.W., and turn left, to 21st St., N.W.

② The Phillips Collection (see pp. 136–137) A small house museum with big-bang exhibits, both permanent and temporary. Backtrack down 21st St., N.W., to Massachusetts Ave., N.W., and turn right.

③ Anderson House (see pp. 131–132) Learn about the Society of the Cincinnati, the secretive patriotic organization whose first president general was none other than George Washington, in this unassuming mansion. Continue up Massachusetts Ave., N.W., and turn right on S St., N.W.

④ President Woodrow Wilson House (see p. 132) See inside one of the neighborhood's poshest homes, and learn about the 28th president at the same time. Continue east on S St., N.W., to 14th St., N.W., and turn left (though there are interesting things to see to the right as well).

⑤ 14th Street, N.W.
(see pp. 132–133) Shop, eat, and drink your way through this booming area between Rhode Island Ave. and U St., N.W., then amble north to U St., N.W.

**DUPONT CIRCLE & BEYOND DISTANCE: 2.5 MILES (4 KM)
TIME: APPROX. 5 HOURS METRO: DUPONT CIRCLE**

Dupont Circle

1 Standing in the midst of tree-shaded Dupont Circle, a pocket-size green haven surrounded by the whiz of traffic, you get a glimpse of L'Enfant's vision of public space—a gift to the citizens of a fledgling democratic nation. Indeed, Dupont Circle is a magnificent meeting space for an egalitarian cross section of suits, uniforms, jeans, and cutoffs. In the middle rises the majestic marble fountain sculpted in 1921 by Daniel Chester French (also known for the giant statue of Lincoln in his memorial on the National Mall). A central column supporting the upper basin is surrounded by three allegorical figures representing the sea, wind, and stars. Honoring Civil War naval hero Samuel Francis du Pont, the fountain replaced a statue of du Pont that originally stood there. Grab a cup to go from a nearby coffee emporium and enjoy some of the city's finest people-watching, or take advantage of the built-in

Intricately woven tapestries line an upstairs hallway of the sumptuous Anderson House, longtime home to the Society of the Cincinnati.

chessboard tables and grassy plots under trees, an open invitation for lounging. Nearby, **Kramerbooks & Afterwords Café** *(1517 Connecticut Ave., N.W., tel 202-387-3825)* is a favorite local bookstore worth some good browsing time.

Intersection of Massachusetts Ave., N.W., Connecticut Ave., N.W., New Hampshire Ave., N.W., P St., N.W., & 19th St., N.W. • Metro: Dupont Circle

The Phillips Collection

2 See pp. 136–137.

1600 21st St., N.W. • tel 202-387-2151 • phillipscollection.org • closed Mon. • $$$ • Metro: Dupont Circle

Anderson House

3 Enter this enormous 1905, 50-room mansion—once called a "Florentine villa in the midst of American independence"— and you enter another world. It was once the winter residence of diplomat Larz Anderson III; his heiress wife, Isabel Weld Perkins, gave the mansion to the Society of the Cincinnati, of which he was a member, upon his death in 1937. It now serves as the society's headquarters and museum. Strolling through the richly decorated rooms, showcasing a mix of artifacts related to the society and the Andersons' outstanding fine and decorative arts collection, you learn the story of this fraternal patriotic organization, dating from 1783. Today's 3,500 members descend from officers in the Continental Army or Navy—indeed, the first president general was George Washington himself.

On the **first floor** you'll find walnut choir stalls dating from 16th-century Italy as well as a two-story-high ballroom with red Verona marble columns. Off the ballroom, a sun-drenched winter salon opens onto a walled garden. On the **second floor** Flemish tapestries in both the luxurious French drawing room and the formal dining room are among the many treasures adorning the walls.

IN **THE KNOW**

Washington's art scene has been stealthily gaining strength, with galleries flourishing all over town. Get to know Dupont Circle's ring of galleries the first Friday of every month when their doors open to all, live music and wine included. Start and end at the **Hillyer Art Space** *(8 Hillyer Ct., N.W.).*

DUPONT CIRCLE & BEYOND

President Wilson addressing the crowd outside his home on Armistice Day, 1922

Historians note: The 40,000-title research library focuses on the art of 18th-century warfare.

2118 Massachusetts Ave., N.W. • tel 202-785-2040 • societyofthecincinnati.org • closed Mon. • Metro: Dupont Circle

President Woodrow Wilson House

4 Get a peek inside another neighborhood home at this lovely Georgian Revival mansion, where the 28th president lived for the three years before his death in 1924. His widow, Edith Bolling Galt Wilson, lived here until her death in 1961, then bequeathing the house—along with much of its furnishings, portraits, books, and artifacts related to the Wilson Administration—to the National Trust for Historic Preservation. Today it appears much as it did when the Wilsons resided here, complete with Woodrow's walking sticks and Edith's gowns in their closets. The artillery shell on his bedroom mantel is said to be the first fired by American forces in World War I.

2340 S St., N.W. • tel 202-387-4062 • woodrowwilsonhouse.org • closed Mon. year-round & Tues.–Thurs. in winter; by guided tour only, on the hour • $$ • Metro: Dupont Circle

14th Street, N.W.

5 The best part about 14th Street is checking out the latest and greatest along the corridor of bars, restaurants, boutiques, antique shops, and theaters between Rhode Island Avenue and U Street on this, one of D.C.'s most happening streets. National names in fashion, cuisine, and theater are also drawn here. Just wander, poke your head into doorways, and see what you come

DUPONT CIRCLE & BEYOND

across. Shopping is fun and funky at **Home Rule** *(1807 14th St., N.W., tel 202-797-5544)*, full of bath and kitchen goodies. **Redeem** *(1810 14th St., N.W., tel 202-332-7447)* offers forward-trending fashion from designers around the world. And **Miss Pixie's** *(1626 14th St., N.W., tel 202-232-8171)* has bookshelves plus silver and textiles and other treasures bought directly at auction.

For eats, the Gulf-style **Pearl Dive Oyster Palace** *(1612 14th St., N.W., tel 202-319-1612)* gives you oysters any way imaginable; the Black Salts are grown specially in Virginia for chef Jeff Black. **B Too** *(1324 14th St., N.W., tel 202-627-2800)* is a hopping contemporary Belgian restaurant that goes above and beyond the standard endive salad and waffles. The ever popular **Le Diplomate** *(1601 14th St., N.W., tel 202-332-3333)*, a quintessential Parisian-style bistro slash café, is chef Stephen Starr's entrée to 14th Street, with great people-watching on the patio. And then there's aviation-themed **Café Saint-Ex** *(1847 14th St., N.W., tel 202-265-7839)*, one of the neighborhood's longest standing ventures (founded in 2003). Named for Antoine de Saint-Exupéry, an avid pilot and author of *Le Petit Prince,* the down-to-earth eatery is French in look, but with a decidedly eclectic Americana menu.

14th St., N.W., bet. Rhode Island Ave. & U St. • Metro: U Street–African-American Civil War Memorial–Cardozo

U Street, N.W.

6 Another hopping street scene, U Street is experiencing phoenix-like growth in an area that deteriorated after the 1968 riots following Martin Luther King's assassination. Before then, in the late 19th and early 20th centuries, this was a prestigious address, home to the city's leading black intellectuals and professionals. People donned their finest attire to frequent the restaurants, movie theaters, pool halls, and dance halls

GOOD **EATS**

See also individual entries.

■ **HANK'S OYSTER BAR**
A longtime neighborhood favorite, with an ever changing oyster menu. **1624 Q St., N.W., tel 202-462-4265, $$–$$$**

■ **LAURIOL PLAZA**
Popular, three-level Tex-Mex restaurant, with Latin American and Spanish added to the mix. **1835 18th St., N.W., tel 202-387-0035, $$**

■ **TABARD INN RESTAURANT**
New American cuisine in an old town house. **1739 N St., N.W., tel 202-785-1277, $$$**

of Black Broadway and be entertained by such local stars as Edward Kennedy "Duke" Ellington and Pearl Bailey. Pay homage to these sights, clustered in and around the junction of 14th Street and U Street, N.W., and enjoy some of the offbeat shops along the way. **Cultural Tourism DC** *(1211 U St., N.W., culturaltourismdc.org)* offers guided heritage walking tours of the neighborhood; stop by their office next to Ben's Chili Bowl.

Other neighborhood highlights include the **African American Civil War Memorial and Museum** *(Memorial: U St. & Vermont Ave., N.W.; Museum: 1925 Vermont Ave., N.W., tel 202-667-2667, afroamcivilwar.org, museum closed Mon.),* dedicated to the African-American troops who fought in the Union Army; exhibits at the museum include photos, newspaper articles, and reproductions of period clothing, uniforms, and weaponry. Big-name gigs have returned to the beautifully restored **Lincoln Theatre** *(1215 U St., N.W., tel 202-888-0050, thelincolndc.com),* dating from 1935. And don't forget to stop by **Ben's Chili Bowl** *(1213 U St., N.W., tel 202-667-0909, benschilibowl.com)* next door for a late-night cup of famous chili. This spicy dog and chili joint—seemingly the only place that has stayed the same through the neighborhood's radical changes—has been a frequent stop since 1958 for those in the know, including such celebrities as Duke Ellington, Bono, and President Barack Obama.

U St., N.W., bet. 9th & 18th Sts. • Metro: Shaw–Howard U, U Street–African-American Civil War Memorial–Cardozo

Adams Morgan

7 This down-to-earth, energetic neighborhood centering on the junction of Columbia Road with 18th Street, N.W., unveils a culturally diverse mélange of noteworthy offerings: from Ethiopian restaurants to salsa bars to global boutiques. Long a Latino enclave and a popular late-night drinking venue among young Washingtonians, the neighborhood has been reinventing itself into a more chichi, craft-cocktail type of destination. That said,

enough of the multicultural character still remains. Grab a cup of coffee at a European-style café, peruse one of the many art galleries and small shops, and take your pick of places to dine on international cuisine. If you're lucky to be here during the Adams Morgan Day Festival on the second Sunday of September (see p. 140), you'll get an insider's look at what it's all about. Favorite hangouts for locals and visitors alike include **Perry's** (*1811 Columbia Rd., N.W., tel 202-234-6218, perrysam.com*), a Japanese restaurant with coveted

A lively food scene flavors Adams Morgan.

rooftop bar and popular Sunday drag-queen brunch; **Songbyrd** (*2477 18th St., N.W., tel 202-450-2917, songbyrddc.com*), purveyors of vinyl music; and **District of Columbia Arts Center** (*2438 18th St., N.W., tel 202-462-7833, dcartscenter.org, closed Mon.–Tues.*), an art gallery for up-and-coming artists that also hosts a theater. If you're still hungry, **Mintwood Place** (*1813 Columbia Rd., N.W., tel 202-234-6732, mintwoodplace.com*) is a foodie destination, with **Julia's Empanadas** (*2452 18th St., N.W., tel 202-328-6232, julias empanadas.com*) being a walk-in favorite.

And if you come here for the nightlife, be sure to check out **Jack Rose Dining Saloon** (*2007 18th St., N.W., tel 202-588-7388, jackrose diningsaloon.com*), a high-end bar noted for its whiskeys; the unforgettably named **Madam's Organ** (*2461 18th St., N.W., tel 202-667-5370, madamsorgan.com*), a lively blues bar and soul food restaurant; and **Habana Village** (*1834 Columbia Rd., N.W., tel 202-462-6310, habana village.com*), with salsa lessons offered most days for a modest fee.

Intersection of Columbia Rd. & 18th St., N.W. • Metro: Woodley Park–Zoo–Adams Morgan

The Phillips Collection

World-class masterpieces in a welcoming space await art lovers at America's first museum of modern art.

The Phillips's oak-paneled Music Room has hosted Sunday afternoon concerts since 1941.

This delightful small museum, which art patron Duncan Phillips established in 1921 based on his personal collection, reigns as the nation's first modern art museum. Intimate rooms occupying Phillips's 1897 Georgian Revival brownstone and a contemporary addition showcase works by Cézanne, van Gogh, Picasso, Gauguin, Klee, and others—with the most celebrated piece being Renoir's dazzling "Luncheon of the Boating Party." But Phillips collected lesser known artists as well—you'll discover them interspersed throughout.

■ SPECIAL EXHIBITS
The Phillips curates blockbuster temporary exhibitions. Start your visit on the third floor with the latest show.

■ RENOIR'S MASTERPIECE
A small set of stairs leads to the room holding Pierre-Auguste Renoir's famous "Luncheon of the Boating Party," an explosion of light and color. Phillips fell in love with the painting   and paid $125,000 in 1923, at a time when seven-room homes in Georgetown sold for $6,500.

■ LAIB'S ROOM OF WAX
Nearby, a single bulb hangs in a small gold-hued room covered with fragrant beeswax, the creation of conceptual artist Wolfgang Laib.

■ A ROOM FULL OF ROTHKO
The Rothko Room was designed to the precise aesthetic specifications of both the abstract expressionist Rothko and Phillips—a rare collaboration between artist and patron. Four large paintings featuring Rothko's signature rectangles of color hang here, enveloping viewers in a saturation of hues.

■ LAWRENCE'S "MIGRATION SERIES"
The Phillips owns the odd numbered paintings of Jacob Lawrence's "Migration Series," which depict the migration of African Americans from the rural South to the urban North during and after World War I. The paintings are moved around the museum, so keep an eye out for them.

■ MUSIC ROOM
A perennial favorite, this oak paneled room with its decorative ceiling and carved mantelpiece has hosted Sunday afternoon concerts since 1941 (*Oct. May; seating first-come, first-served*).

■ A BIT OF FRESH AIR
Before leaving, take a rest on the benches of the outdoor courtyard as you ponder the open-air sculptures.

DUPONT CIRCLE & BEYOND

1600 21st St., N.W. • tel 202-387-2151 • phillipscollection.org • closed Mon., Sunday p.m. concerts Oct.–May • $$$ • Metro: Dupont Circle

Multicultural Washington

You could say Washington was created by a French man. Indeed, Pierre-Charles L'Enfant is responsible for the noble, tree-shaded, Euro-style urban design that graces the nation's capital—roundabouts, broad boulevards, lots of fountains and statues, stone buildings, and a grand parklike mall included. Since those early days, Washington has welcomed people from around the world—foreign delegations, of course, but also others in search of a better way of life, bringing with them their cultures, cuisines, and traditions.

Drumming at Meridian Park (above) and international restaurants (opposite) are but two of the hundreds of ways that Washington's ethnic diversity is celebrated and shared with residents and visitors alike.

In the Beginning

L'Enfant aside, Washington was not so ethnically diverse in the beginning. Indeed, in 1900, only 7 percent of the population was foreign-born, compared to New York's 37 percent, Boston's 35 percent, and Philadelphia's 23 percent. Today, about 1 in 7 Washingtonians are foreign-born.

Abroad at Home

Throughout the Washington area, you'll find neighborhoods where various ethnic groups have settled, establishing shops, restaurants, and businesses to support their communities, celebrating traditions and annual festivals—and offering a way for everyone to experience the world at home.

Chinatown is one of the oldest neighborhoods, established in the 1930s. Restaurants and shops cluster in the hopping Penn Quarter neighborhood, where a colorful Friendship Arch spans over H Street and the Chinese New Year parade unfurls.

The years following the Vietnam War saw an influx in Vietnamese. The Eden Center strip mall in the D.C. suburb of Falls Church, Virginia, offers 100-plus Vietnamese bakeries, restaurants, groceries, and shops. An annual Tet Festival attracts thousands with food, fireworks, live entertainment, and lion dances.

Washington boasts what is believed to be the world's second largest Ethiopian population, after Addis Ababa; many Ethiopians sought asylum in the United States as a result of Ethiopia's civil war in the 1990s. Little Ethiopia is found along U Street between 13th and 9th Streets, N.W. Among Latinos, you'll find every Central and South American country represented throughout the Washington region, with El Salvadoreans claiming the highest representation. Adams Morgan is historically the heart of the Latino community, where you'll still find *pupuserias* and salsa clubs. And the list goes on and on.

INTERNATIONAL
RESTAURANTS

Here are some of D.C.'s best ethnic restaurants.
Acadiana (Cajun/Creole)
901 New York Ave., N.W.,
tel 202-408-8848
Bombay Club (Indian)
815 Connecticut Ave., N.W.,
tel 202-659-3727
Brasserie Beck (Belgian)
1101 K St., N.W.,
tel 202-408-1717
**Dukem Ethiopian
Restaurant,** 1114–1118 U St.,
N.W., tel 202-667-8735
Lebanese Taverna
2641 Connecticut Ave., N.W.,
tel 202-265-8681
Mandu (Korean) 1805 18th
St., N.W., tel 202-588-1540
Mari Vanna (Russian)
1141 Connecticut Ave., N.W.,
tel 202-783-7777

World of Festivals

Experience Washington's tapestry of different cultures, celebrated throughout the year with extravagant music, parades, dance, and—always—lots of good food.

■ ADAMS MORGAN DAY

Since 1978, on the second Sunday of September, the streets of the traditionally Latino Adams Morgan are blocked off for the eclectic neighborhood festival, complete with live music, international food, and an **International Dance Plaza** featuring all kinds of dance performances, including Bolivian and Mexican folk—and the chance to learn some basic moves yourself.

18th St., N.W., bet. Florida Ave. & Columbia Rd. • second Sun. in Sept.

■ DRAGON BOAT FESTIVAL

Vibrantly colored dragon boats race on the Potomac River in an ancient Chinese tradition that also includes cultural exhibits, food, and music. The two-day festivities kick off with the **Eye-dotting Ceremony** to awaken the sleeping dragon boats. For the best vantages, head to the Washington Harbour and Georgetown Riverfront Park.

Thompson Boat Ctr., 2900 Virginia Ave., N.W. • tel 202-333-9543 • dragonboatdc.com • May

■ FIESTA DC

This annual extravaganza of Latino heritage has become so big that it's been moved downtown from the Columbia Heights neighborhood. The highlight is the **Parade of Nations,** featuring more than 30 folkloric groups from Spain, Latin America, and Mexico sashaying down Constitution Avenue. Other **Festival Latino** events include a children's festival, science fair, and plenty of international cuisine.

Parade of Nations: Constitution Ave., N.W., bet. 7th & 14th Sts.; Festival Latino: Pennsylvania Ave., N.W., between 9th & 14th Sts. • tel 202-489-7141 • fiestadc.org • Sept.

■ ST. PATRICK'S DAY PARADE

Bagpipers—plus 100 marching bands, military units, dance schools, floats, and more—march down Constitution Avenue in this enormous annual tradition going on for more than 45 years. Grandstand tickets are available for a price.

Constitution Ave., N.W., bet. 7th & 17th Sts. • tel 202-670-0317 • dcstpatsparade.com • Sun. near St. Patrick's Day

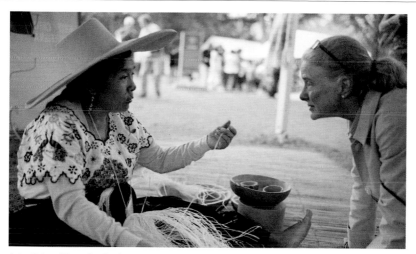

A traditional Peruvian basket weaver shares stories at the Smithsonian Folklife Festival.

▪ NATIONAL CHERRY BLOSSOM FESTIVAL

A four-week celebration with the famous blooms as its centerpiece. See pp. 64–65 for more information.

Tidal Basin & surrounds • tel 877-442-5666 • nationalcherryblossomfestival.org

▪ SMITHSONIAN FOLKLIFE FESTIVAL

The Smithsonian's Center for Folklife and Cultural Heritage spotlights several different cultures from around the world in this massive, dynamic festival on the National Mall. Hundreds of artisans, chefs, musicians, and storytellers entertain thousands with demonstrations, talks, and concerts, with overall themes and countries highlighted each year. Try to arrive early to avoid the crowds; it's always hot—drink plenty of water.

National Mall • tel 202-633-6440 • festival .si.edu • weekends nearest Fourth of July

▪ SCOTTISH CHRISTMAS WALK WEEKEND

Hundreds of Scottish clansmen with tartans and bagpipes parade through Old Town Alexandria in this annual December event. Other activities include a historic homes tour, a Celtic party, and Christmas marketplace.

King St., Old Town Alexandria • tel 703-549-0111 • campagnacenter.org • first Sat. in Dec.

Georgetown

Centering on Gothic-spired Georgetown University, Washington's superchic neighborhood mixes posh shopping and energetic nightlife with quiet streets lined by refined federal and Victorian architecture. It began as a tobacco inspection shipment port on the highest navigable point along the Potomac River. The colony of Maryland established a town here in the 1750s, naming it for George II. Georgetown became a thriving trade center, with stately merchant houses spangling the hill, and artisans' shops and warehouses along the riverside. Georgetown's blacksmiths, cabinet-makers, carpenters, and other artisans supported the fledgling Federal City with materials to build the White House and other federal buildings in the late 1700s. The city of Washington annexed Georgetown in 1871. Among the busy shops and restaurants you'll find such historic landmarks as the C & O Canal and Old Stone House, along with genteel manses and lovingly maintained gardens that provide a glimpse into yesteryear, Tudor Place, and Dumbarton House among them.

◀ **The Chesapeake and Ohio (C & O) Canal** stretches some 184.5 miles (297 km) from Cumberland, Maryland, to Washington, D.C., passing through Georgetown. Its scenic towpath is much enjoyed by locals.

Georgetown

Brick row houses along tree-shaded streets, pocket gardens, and award-winning eateries are just a few of the charms of this historic neighborhood.

7 Tudor Place Historic House & Garden (see p. 149) Six generations of the same family lived here. Continue up 31st St., N.W., turn left on R St., N.W., and right on 32nd St., N.W.

8 Dumbarton Oaks (see pp. 152–153) This historic house has a hidden gem of a museum, plus formal gardens designed by landscape architect Beatrix Farrand. Backtrack on R St., N.W.

6 Cox's Row & Around (see p. 149) Admire more stately federal homes on a picturesque cobbled street. Continue on N St., N.W., to 31st St., N.W., and turn left to Q St., N.W.

5 Georgetown University (see p. 148) Stroll the grounds of America's first Catholic university, dating from 1789. Exiting campus, turn right on 37th and left on N St., N.W., to 34th St., N.W.

Georgetown University 5

O ST.

Q ST.

P ST.

N ST.

STREET · STREET

6 Cox's Row & Around

33RD

35TH

36TH ST.

37TH ST.

34TH

← **To Kreeger Museum**

CANAL ROAD

C & O Canal Towpath

CHESAPEAKE & OHIO CANAL NATIONAL HISTORICAL PARK

Prospect Street

M STREET

FRANCIS SCOTT KEY PARK

FRANCIS SCOTT KEY MEMORIAL BRIDGE

GEORGETOWN WATERFRONT PARK

D.C. VA.

To U.S. Naval Observatory

RESERVOIR RD.

4 Prospect Street, N.W. (see pp. 147–148) Gaze at gorgeous historic homes. Turn right at 37th St., N.W., to O St., N.W., and the entrance to Georgetown University.

GEORGETOWN DISTANCE: 3.3 MILES (5.3 KM)
TIME: APPROX. 6 HOURS METRO: FOGGY BOTTOM–GWU

GEORGETOWN

Dumbarton Oaks

MONTROSE PARK

Oak Hill Chapel & Cemetery

R ST.

Tudor Place Historic House & Garden ⑦

8

32ND ST.
31ST ST.

Rock Creek

9 Oak Hill Chapel & Cemetery (see p. 150) The final resting place of some of Washington's most famous movers and shakers. Continue on R St., wrapping around to 28th St., N.W., then turning left on Q St., N.W.

⑩ Dumbarton House (see pp. 150–151) A fascinating glimpse into Georgetown's early history through the eyes of one family. Attend an evening concert or other special event in the historic house.

Dumbarton House
10

Q ST.

Q ST.

P ST.
30TH ST.
29TH ST.

1 Old Stone House (see p. 146) Visit Washington's oldest house, then head down Thomas Jefferson St., N.W., to the canal, and turn left.

WISCONSIN AVENUE

O ST.

St. John's Church

Martin's Tavern

N ST.

GEORGETOWN

PROSPECT STREET

Old Stone House

M STREET

The Shops at Georgetown Park

Blues Alley

WISCONSIN AVE.

Georgetown Visitor Center for C & O Canal

Chesapeake & Ohio Canal

GRACE ST.

31ST ST.

T. JEFFERSON ST.

CHESAPEAKE & OHIO CANAL NATIONAL HISTORICAL PARK

SOUTH ST.

CECIL PL.

(29)

WHITEHURST FWY. (elevated)

Potomac

GEORGETOWN WATERFRONT PARK

3 Washington Harbour

30TH ST.

Rock Creek

Thompson Boat Center

0 ────── 200 meters
0 ────── 200 yards

2 Chesapeake & Ohio Canal National Historical Park (see p. 146) After stopping by the Georgetown Visitor Center, head west along this 184.5-mile (297 km) historic towpath. In summer you can take a mule-drawn barge ride. Stroll to 31st St., N.W., and turn left to Washington Harbour.

3 Washington Harbour (see p. 147) Bustling restaurants and bars with a riverside view—this is the perfect place for lunch. Walk north along Georgetown Waterfront Park to 34th St, N.W., up the steps, over the canal, then up through Francis Scott Key Park. Crossing M St., N.W., go left to 35th St., N.W., and walk up the steep hill

Old Stone House

1 Washington's oldest house (dating from 1765), the Old Stone House has through the years served as a house painter's shop, clockmaker's shop, antiques store, and the offices of a used-car dealership. The legend that George Washington slept here—though since disproved—helped keep it from demolition. The federal government bought the house in 1953 to preserve its history, and today it provides a glimpse into ordinary Georgetown life before the founding of the Capital City. Poke your head inside to see the kitchen, parlor, and bedrooms furnished as in the late 18th century. Out back, a colonial revival garden contains roses, perennials, and bulbs.

3051 M St., N.W. • tel 202-895-6070 • nps.gov/olst • Metro: Foggy Bottom–GWU

Chesapeake & Ohio Canal National Historical Park

2 George Washington dreamed of a canal that would connect the Atlantic coast with the Ohio River and he was the first president of the Patowmack Company, organized in 1785. Bankrupt, the Patowmack was succeeded in 1828 by the C & O, which built a canal as far as Cumberland, Maryland, and used it to transport grains, tobacco, whiskey, furs, and timber until railroads drove it out of business in the early 20th century. Thanks in large part to the conservationist clout of Supreme Court Justice William O. Douglas, the canal was saved from death by highway in the 1950s. Today it's a beautiful national historical park, a long, skinny recreation area that gets wilder the farther northwest you go—you can hike, bike, or walk the entire 184.5 miles (297 km) to Cumberland, though a short wander will also give you a nice respite. Stop at the **Visitor Center** in Georgetown for a free walking tour of the neighborhood or an hour-long ride in a reproduction of a **canal boat** from the 1800s—pulled by live mules!—that combines a pleasant excursion with a narrative on the canal's history and construction.

Visitor center: 1057 Thomas Jefferson St., N.W. • tel 202-653-5190 • nps.gov/choh • canal rides: seasonal; visitor center: closed winter • canal ride: $ • Metro: Foggy Bottom–GWU

Enjoying a meal at Washington Harbour, where Georgetown meets the Potomac River

Washington Harbour

3 In warm weather, this wide promenade hugging the Potomac River's northern shore becomes a prime Georgetown hot spot. Stop for lunch or a drink in an open-air restaurant (Sequoia is one of the more popular, with a tree-shaded terrace); or relax on a bench to enjoy close-up views of the river as well as leafy Roosevelt Island (dead ahead) and the sleek Kennedy Center (to the left). Just north along the Potomac, **Georgetown Waterfront Park** offers a beautiful riverside stroll toward the Key Bridge's graceful arches.

3050 K St., N.W. • tel 202-295-5007 • thewashingtonharbour.com • Metro: Foggy Bottom–GWU

Prospect Street, N.W.

4 This lovely, tree-shaded street boasts some of Georgetown's oldest and most fashionable houses, dating back to a time when wealthy ship owners, merchants, and land speculators built mansions above the three-masted-schooner-filled harbor. At the corner of 34th

GEORGETOWN

IN **THE KNOW**

Georgetown's chic row houses have long been coveted by the rich and famous. Jacqueline and John F. Kennedy are perhaps the most celebrated residents—JFK had seven Georgetown addresses until moving into 3307 N St., N.W., with Jackie; from here they went on to the White House. Elizabeth Taylor, as wife of Senator John Warner, lived at 3240 S St., N.W. Julia Child resided on Olive Street, N.W. There are plenty of high-level officials living on these leafy streets today; their addresses are unpublished, but the Secret Service agents standing guard are a dead giveaway.

and Prospect, No. 3400 identifies the federal-style **Halcyon House** (1787) built by Benjamin Stoddert, a Revolutionary War hero and the first secretary of the Navy. It served as a center of the young capital's social life—Dolley Madison danced here at the wedding of Stoddert's daughter. Today it serves as a creative space for 21st-century problem solvers. A few houses away stands **Worthington House** (No. 3425), built in 1798 by prominent landholder John Thomson Mason; the 24-paned windows lining both main floors cost a mint at the time. Just past 35th Street, at No. 3508, **Prospect House** (1788–1793) is a late Georgian beauty built by a Revolutionary War officer and outspoken advocate of freedom of the press.

Prospect St., N.W., bet. 34th & 35th Sts. • All private • Metro: Foggy Bottom–GWU

Georgetown University

5 When Georgetown opened in 1789, it was the United States' first Catholic university. The Gothic-spired university is best known for its schools of law, medicine, and foreign service (and its basketball team). Through the main gate you'll see **Healy Hall,** the historic flagship building named after Father Patrick Healy, an African-American priest and president of Georgetown in the 1870s. Note the hands on the clock tower, the object of many student pranks over time. Every five or six years (or whenever they can pull off the stunt), students steal these hands and mail them to the Vatican; the Vatican simply stamps "return to sender" and the package is returned to the university. Filled with students, the 104-acre (42 ha) campus is a pleasant place for a stroll; permanent maps sprinkled about the grounds help guide the way.

3700 O St., N.W. • tel 202-687-0100 • georgetown.edu • Metro: Foggy Bottom–GWU

Cox's Row & Around

6 Col. John Cox, the future mayor of Georgetown, built this grouping of stately federal-style brick town houses (*3327 to 3339 N St., N.W.*) around 1818. Cox entertained the Marquis de Lafayette at **No. 3337** during his U.S. visit in 1824. John F. and Jackie Kennedy lived at **No. 3307** between 1957 and 1961, before moving into the White House.

3300 block of N St., N.W. • Metro: Foggy Bottom–GWU

The pleasing facades of Cox's Row are little changed since their construction in the 19th century.

Tudor Place
Historic House & Garden

7 Six generations of the Peter family—relatives of George Washington and Robert E. Lee—resided in this grand neoclassical mansion, which looks as if the family is still living here. Indeed, all of the furniture, porcelain, and decorative objects are original, reflecting the family's 178-year continuity between 1805 and 1983. Personal belongings include 253 pieces from Mount Vernon (look for the chairs from George's war headquarters and Martha's tea table), an etching of the Marquis de Lafayette that he himself presented when he was entertained here, and Francis Scott Key's desk. One-hour tours by experienced guides provide fascinating details about the Peter family, as well an overview of the architect—William Thornton, first architect of the U.S. Capitol, who incorporated a rare, full "temple" into the two-story stuccoed main building. Be sure to leave time to visit the gardens (see p. 156), which are among Georgetown's loveliest.

1644 31st St., N.W. • tel 202-965-0400 • tudorplace.org • by guided tour only, on the hour; closed Mon. & Jan. • $$ • Metro: Foggy Bottom–GWU

Dumbarton Oaks

8 See pp. 152–153.

Museum: 1703 32nd St., N.W.; Gardens entrance: R St. at 31st St., N.W.
• tel 202-339-6401 • doaks.org • Museum: closed a.m. & Mon.; Gardens: closed
Nov.–mid-March & a.m. • gardens: $$ • Metro: Foggy Bottom–GWU, Dupont Circle

Oak Hill Chapel & Cemetery

9 One of the prettiest cemeteries anywhere, on a hillside over-
looking Rock Creek Park, Oak Hill is the final resting place for
some of Washington's greatest notables, including former Secretary
of State Dean Acheson as well as Phillip and Katharine Graham
(former publishers of the *Washington Post*). There are doctors,
lawyers, politicians, and generals galore, as well as a Confederate spy
or two. Founded in 1849 by philanthropist and art collector William
Wilson Corcoran (who's also buried here), its iron entrance gates
and English Gothic Revival chapel were designed by James Renwick,
architect of the Smithsonian Castle. Buy a map at the gatehouse.

3001 R St., N.W. • tel 202-337-2835 • oakhillcemeterydc.org • Metro: Foggy
Bottom–GWU, Dupont Circle

GOOD **EATS**

■ **1789 RESTAURANT**
Fine dining in a federal period
town house. **1226 36th St.,
N.W., tel 202-965-1789, $$$$$**

■ **BOOEYMONGER**
Creative sandwiches are the
hallmark of this local chain.
**3256 Prospect St., N.W., tel
202-333-4810, $**

■ **MARTIN'S TAVERN**
The oldest family-run restau-
rant in Washington, D.C., since
1933. **1264 Wisconsin Ave.,
N.W., tel 202-333-7230,
$$–$$$**

Dumbarton House

10 A meticulously and lovingly restored tribute
to early Georgetown, this federal-style
house-museum (built in 1800) tells the story
of the 1804–1813 time period through the eyes
of a local family. Joseph Nourse, who worked as
the Register of the Treasury in the new federal
government, moved here from Philadelphia with
his wife when Georgetown had just been incorpo-
rated into the District of Columbia. Treasures
abound throughout the mansion, but perhaps
what is most amazing is the thoroughness of the
restoration—the historic accuracy of the carpeting,
the window dressings, the wallpaper, all

GEORGETOWN

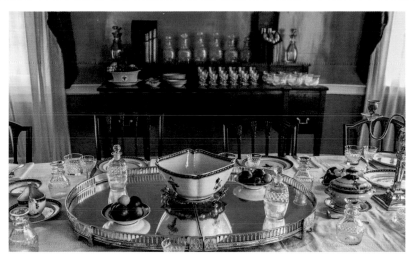

Dumbarton House's Chinese export blue-and-white porcelain dinner service dates from 1790.

reproduced based on original research, matching styles, colors, and methods of the day (and yes, early Americans did love their colors so bright!).

Keep an eye out for several outstanding artifacts, including Charles Willson Peale's painting "The Benjamin Stoddert Children" (1789) in the breakfast room, its background depicting early Georgetown; the porcelain dinner service that once belonged to Martha Washington's granddaughter in the dining room; and the rare schoolgirl needlework in the parlor. The second floor contains four galleries, one exploring the story of the National Society of the Colonial Dames of America, which curates the house and is headquartered here. Both self-guided and guided tours are offered; if you have time, a guided tour is highly recommended. After, take the self-guiding brochure for a peek at the small formal courtyard and garden. Special evening concerts happen on occasion; check the website for details.

2715 Q St., N.W. • tel 202-337-2288 • dumbartonhouse.org • by guided & self-guided tour; closed Mon. • $ • Metro: Dupont Circle

Dumbarton Oaks

*Discover the treasures beyond the famous gardens
at this exquisite Georgetown gem.*

Ornate baroque lines grace the pebble garden at Dumbarton Oaks, one of many lovely
botanical displays created by master landscape architect Beatrix Farrand.

Many Washingtonians know—rightly so—about the luxuriant gardens at
Dumbarton Oaks, designed by celebrated landscape architect Beatrix Farrand.
But few take the time to step inside the lavish, federal-style home, where
you'll find one of the world's most important small museums of Byzantine
and pre-Columbian art. Collected by Mildred and Robert Woods Bliss, this
impressive display is now curated by Harvard University. Here, too, the 1944
conference was held to charter the United Nations. The museum is free;
you'll have to buy a ticket to visit the gardens.

■ BYZANTINE COLLECTION

Begin at the **Byzantine Courtyard Gallery** and the adjacent **Byzantine Gallery,** with artifacts spanning the 4th to the 15th centuries. The Blisses were especially captivated by the intricate detail work and fine craftsmanship of small objets d'art, which you'll find reflected in the gold, silver, and bronze vessels used for the celebration of the Eucharist, late Roman and Byzantine jewelry, coins, cloisonné enamels, and illuminated manuscripts. The neighboring **Textile Room** has rotating exhibits.

■ HOUSE COLLECTION

The stately **Music Room,** designed in 1928 by the architectural firm of McKim, Mead & White and displaying a gorgeously painted wood-beamed ceiling, showcases the so-called House Collection. Exquisite tapestries and paintings hang on the walls   including El Greco's **"Visitation"** from the early 17th century. The 1926 **Steinway concert grand piano** is signed by Ignacy Paderewski. An exhibit gives a quick history on the Dumbarton Oaks Conference, which took place in this room.

SAVVY **TRAVELER**

Dumbarton Oaks is a self-guided visit, but a variety of different tours are available for those wanting to dive deeper. Some of the offerings include a **special exhibition** tour, a **historic rooms** tour (including the hall, Founders' Room, Study, and Oval Room), an **architecture tour,** and an **introductory garden tour.** Check *doaks.org* for more details.

■ PRE-COLUMBIAN COLLECTION

A glass-and-travertine wing, inspired by Islamic architecture and designed by Philip Johnson, features circular galleries of glistening display cases arranged by region. These hold treasures from Latin America's ancient cultures, such as sparkling gold pectorals, ceremonial jewelry, and stone carvings of Aztec deities and animals.

■ THE GARDENS

Begin in the orangerie, where an entwining ficus plant from the 1860s festoons the walls and ceiling. Then wander through the gardens—a sweet-smelling realm of brick paths, boxwoods, perennial borders, iron gates, and balconies.

GEORGETOWN

Museum: 1703 32nd St., N.W.; Gardens entrance: R St. at 31st St., N.W. • tel 202-339-6401 • doaks.org • Museum: closed a.m. & Mon.; Gardens: closed Nov.–mid-March & a.m. • Garden: $$ • Metro: Foggy Bottom–GWU, Dupont Circle

Spies Among Us

Intrigue. Mystery. Romance. Spies have captured the imagination of moviegoers and television-watchers for decades. But in Washington—home of the CIA, the FBI, and the Pentagon—such cinematic fare is real, with city streets very possibly alive with secret agents seeking or supplying classified information. Indeed, Washington boasts more spies than any other city in the world. You never know who you can trust!

When Soviet KGB colonel Vitaly Yurchenko (above) returned to the Soviet Union in 1985 after defecting to the United States, many wondered if he was a KGB plant all along. His story, and many others, is told at the International Spy Museum (opposite).

Civil War Espionage

Spying caught on in Washington during the Civil War, when amateur agents on both sides of the Mason–Dixon line scoured the Capital City for war-related information. The city's most romantic spy may have been intelligent, beautiful, and duplicitous Rose O'Neal Greenhow (1815–1864), who frequented Washington's loftiest social circles. At one dinner party, after learning the Federals were planning to move into Virginia, she quickly passed a coded message to Confederate Gen. Pierre G. T. Beauregard inside a woman's hair bun, enabling him to reposition some of his troops—and, ultimately, to win the First Battle of Bull Run.

Cold War Spies & Beyond

Soviet KGB colonel Vitaly Yurchenko made world headlines when he strolled into the U.S. Embassy in Rome in August 1985 and stated he wished to defect. But Yurchenko was not a happy decamper, kept under close watch and relegated to a prisonlike existence. In November Yurchenko slipped his CIA handler and grabbed a cab to the Soviet Embassy. Four days later he was on a plane back to the Soviet Union. Then came Aldrich Ames, who in 1994 was accused of exposing U.S. intelligence assets inside the former Soviet Union. The info swap occurred at the now-defunct Chadwicks, at 3205 K Street in Georgetown; Ames chalkmarked a blue mailbox on R Street at 37th Street as a dead-drop signal. For his tip-offs, Ames received more than $2.7 million from the Soviets—and from the Americans, a life-long prison sentence.

Today spying is largely about tracking terrorist activities—the U.S. keeping tabs on Iran, North Korea, China, and the Islamic State. All of which no doubt are returning the favor.

HOW TO SEE— AND BE—**A SPY**

Carol Bessette, a retired Air Force officer and military intelligence expert, leads special spy walking tours (*spiesofwashingtontour.com*), focusing on tales of intrigue throughout the Capital City. To try your own hand at intelligence activities, check out Operation Spy at the International Spy Museum (see pp. 94–95).

GEORGETOWN

Gardens

Since Washington's earliest days, gardens have always had an important place in homes and public spaces alike—for practical purposes, but for beauty, too. Here are just a few of the beautiful spaces found throughout the city.

In springtime, keep an eye out for garden tours—including at the White House!

GEORGETOWN

■ TUDOR PLACE HISTORIC HOUSE & GARDEN

Tudor Place's quiet acres in the heart of Georgetown represent one of the nation's last intact urban estates from the federal period. Explore the sweeping **South Lawn** framed by 200-year-old trees, a **Box Knot Garden** featuring a "flower knot" pattern of English boxwoods and pathways, and the natural woodland settings. A garden map is available.

1644 31st St., N.W. • tel 202-965-0400
• tudorplace.org • closed Mon. & Jan. • $
• Metro: Foggy Bottom–GWU

■ U.S. BOTANIC GARDEN

Inside the iron-and-glass greenhouse on the Capitol grounds, more than 4,000 seasonal, tropical, and subtropical plants flourish—ranging from pineapple-scented sage to a plant that smells like rotting corpses. Established in 1820 and run by Congress, the garden's role through the ages has been to accumulate plants from military and exploring missions, foreign governments, states, and government agencies. Be sure to climb the stairs to the overhanging walkway in the large tropical atrium, filled with orchids and other epiphytes.

100 Maryland Ave., S.W. • tel 202- 225-8333
• usbg.gov • Metro: Federal Center SW

■ FLORAL LIBRARY

On a site close to the famed cherry blossoms, some 10,000 tulip bulbs are planted by hand, later exploding in a vibrancy of springtime color. They are flown in every year from Holland to represent nearly 100 different varieties, explaining why this is called the Tulip Library as well. The rest of the year, annuals provide a sweet break from urban bustle. Established in 1969, the library was part of Lady Bird Johnson's effort to beautify the Capital City.

Just off Tidal Basin, east of Katz Bridge & south of Independence Ave., S.W. • nps.gov/nama
• Metro: Smithsonian

The Rosary Portico frames the peaceful formal gardens of the Franciscan Monastery.

■ FRANCISCAN MONASTERY
One of Washington's best-kept secrets, tucked away on the grounds of a neo-Byzantine church, this oasis of peace in Northeast's Brookland neighborhood features lovingly executed reproductions of Holy Land shrines—the Grotto of Gethsemane, Chapel of the Ascension, the Tomb of Mary, plus the Lourdes grotto—all amid a parklike garden. Here, too, cloisters enclose a formal rose garden with benches thoughtfully placed for quiet contemplation. Check the website for a blooming calendar and to schedule tours of the monastery.

1400 Quincy St., N.E. • tel 202- 526-6800
• myfranciscan.org • Metro: Brookland–CUA

■ RIVER FARM
Overlooking the Potomac River south of Old Town Alexandria, en route to Mount Vernon, River Farm's landscaped grounds cover property that once belonged to George Washington. Among its meticulously maintained gardens are a small grove of Franklin trees (extinct in the wild), an orchard of pear, apple, and plum trees, and an azalea garden with hundreds of different kinds of azalea species. This beautiful setting is the headquarters of the American Horticultural Society.

7931 E. Boulevard Dr., Alexandria
• tel 703-768-5700 • ahs.org/river_farm
• open Mon.–Fri. April–Sept., plus Sat. a.m.
Oct.–March • Not Metro accessible

OLD TOWN
ALEXANDRIA

Old Town Alexandria

Long before any notion of Washington, D.C., existed, Alexandria, Virginia, was a thriving colonial hotbed, known intimately by such patriots as Paul Revere, Thomas Jefferson, and, of course, nearby Mount Vernon resident George Washington. They worshipped at Christ Church, dined (and imbibed) at Gadsby's Tavern, and some even plotted wartime activity at the Carlyle House. Today, this quiet little realm of brick town houses, cobbled streets, and historic sites, located along the Potomac about 10 miles (16 km) downstream of Washington, is a delightfully strollable destination, easily reachable from D.C. by the Metro's blue line. Here, too, you'll find some of the region's most lauded bars, restaurants, cafés, art galleries, and boutiques—and a buzzing nightlife, especially in summer.

◀ **The former torpedo factory along Alexandria's waterfront is now a thriving arts center where more than 165 artists create, exhibit, and sell their work.**

OLD TOWN ALEXANDRIA

Old Town Alexandria

Older than Washington, charming Old Town Alexandria offers a step back into colonial days.

9 Torpedo Factory Art Center (see p. 169) Visit local potters, painters, and weavers as they purvey their arts and crafts in this former World War II torpedo factory. Then relax with some entertainment on the dock behind, overlooking the Potomac.

George Washington Masonic National Memorial

6

PRINCESS ST.

QUEEN ST.

KING ST.

King Street

CAMERON ST.

1 1

KING STREET

PAYNE STREET

HENRY ST.

PATRICK ST.

DUKE ST.

DUKE ST.

7 Lyceum, Alexandria's History Museum (see pp. 167–168) Get a primer on Alexandria's history, from Native American settlements to the present day. Backtrack to King St., turn right, then right on S. Fairfax St.

8 Stabler-Leadbeater Apothecary Museum (see pp. 168–169) George Washington himself would recognize this pharmacy dating from colonial days. Continue down King St. to the Potomac River.

**OLD TOWN ALEXANDRIA   DISTANCE: 3.45 MILES (5.5 KM)
TIME: 8 HOURS   METRO: KING STREET–OLD TOWN**

OLD TOWN ALEXANDRIA

❶ Alexandria Visitor Center at Ramsay House (see p. 162) Enjoy breakfast at one of King Street's many cafés then begin your walk at this reconstruction of the 1724 home of town founder William Ramsay, now serving as the city's visitor information center. Go north on N. Fairfax St.

0 — 200 meters
0 — 200 yards

❷ Carlyle House Historic Park (see pp. 162–163) Learn about one of Alexandria's earliest families at this colonial-era house, where British generals also plotted their strategy for the French and Indian War. At Cameron St., turn left and walk one block.

❸ Gadsby's Tavern Museum (see pp. 163–164) Visit this historic tavern, then dine at the restaurant as the colonists did. Go north on N. Royal St., then left at Oronoco St.

❹ Lee-Fendall House (see p. 165) Tours provide insight into the Lee family dynasty. Turn left on N. Washington St.

OLD TOWN ALEXANDRIA

❻ George Washington Masonic National Memorial (see pp. 166–167) Admire the view from the top of this majestic temple at the head of King St., where a small museum sheds light on the Masons. Then go back down King St. to N. Washington St. and turn right.

❺ Christ Church (see pp. 170–171) Washington, Jefferson, and other patriots worshipped at this Anglican church. Go ahead and sit in Washington's pew, then exit onto N. Washington St., turn right, then right on King St. Walk the 1.3 miles (2 km) or take a cab to the temple.

OLD TOWN ALEXANDRIA

Alexandria Visitor Center at Ramsay House

1 After enjoying breakfast at one of King Street's many cafés, stop by the city's visitor center for maps and some brochures to help plan your visit. While you're at it, take a good look at the architectural details of this meticulous reconstruction of the circa 1724 home of Scottish merchant and town founder William Ramsay. Be sure to check out special events on offer, including ghost tours and candlelit tours. The "Key to the City" pass available here offers a discount on various museum entry fees.

221 King St., Alexandria • tel 703-746-3301 • visitalexandriava.com • Metro: King St.–Old Town

Carlyle House Historic Park

2 Scottish merchant John Carlyle completed this stone manse in the Georgian style in 1753, when Alexandria consisted mostly of small dwellings and warehouses. Soon, the French and Indian War pitted the British against the French and Indians, and Gen. Edward Braddock requisitioned the house for strategic planning with five colonial governors—he went on to be killed in battle in Pennsylvania. Today, guided tours begin every half-hour with an introduction providing historical context into the life and times of the Carlyle family. You will be greeted by your tour guide in the central passage (the best place in the house to catch a cool breeze in summer) and travel back in time to the 18th century. The first floor offers the main bedchamber, which has three original pieces of furniture, including a majestic four-poster bed and a lovely 1750 chest. Nearby is Carlyle's study, where he ran his mercantile business and which served as a private family space as well. You'll be taken through the parlor and formal dining room before heading up the main staircase to the second floor. Life in early America unveils itself with such details as the spinet harpsichord, similar to one played by Carlyle's daughter (who took lessons at Mount Vernon); fancy dinner place settings; and the popular green wallpaper so à la mode in the day (you'll find it at Mount Vernon and Dumbarton

Shops and restaurants vie for attention on Alexandria's King Street.

House as well). Exhibits on the second floor convey the life and times of various eras in Carlyle House's history, such as during the Civil War, when it was subsumed into a Union hospital known as Mansion House Hospital. Don't miss artifacts on display belonging to the real-life characters who inspired the public television series "Mercy Street," which delves into the everyday lives of Alexandrians during the Civil War.

121 N. Fairfax St., Alexandria • tel 703-549-2997 • nvrpa.org • $ • by guided tour only; closed Mon. • Metro: King St.–Old Town

Gadsby's Tavern Museum

3 Step into this beautifully preserved colonial-era public house and you might very well expect to find Thomas Jefferson, John Adams, James Madison, or any number of other early patriots imbibing as they discuss the social, political, and economic issues of

OLD TOWN ALEXANDRIA

IN **THE KNOW**

As you walk from Gadsby's Tavern to the Lee-Fendall House, keep an eye out for the **"Spite House"** at 523 Queen St. The skinniest house in America, it measures just 7 feet (2 m) wide! John Hollensbury built it in 1830 to keep loiterers out of his adjacent alley.

the day. It's known that George Washington would stop here between trips to and from his home at Mount Vernon. Consisting of a 1785 tavern and a 1792 hotel, Gadsby's has been faithfully restored as a museum and operating restaurant. The 30-minute tour takes you to the taproom, dining room, ballroom, assembly room, and third-floor communal bedchambers. As you admire the beautifully reproduced woodwork in the ballroom, remember that George Washington was honored here at the annual Birthnight Ball in 1798 and 1799; that Thomas Jefferson celebrated his inaugural banquet here in 1801; and that the Marquis de Lafayette was welcomed here on his American visit in 1824, at what was heralded as "one of the most brilliant of banquets." A visit to the period **Gadsby's Tavern Restaurant** *(138 N. Royal St., tel 703-548-1288)* may bring peanut soup, Gentleman's Pye (lamb and beef in a red-wine stew topped with whipped potatoes and pastry crust), what's called George Washington's favorite (grilled breast of duck with scalloped potatoes and corn pudding), and other colonial-era specialties. Outside, peer into the subterranean ice well, built to assure a regular supply of ice—and year-round ice cream with flavors including vanilla, oyster, and parmesan; the dark paving stones on the corner of Royal and Cameron Streets mark the well's perimeter. En route to your next stop, take a glance at the frame house standing a block west at **508 Cameron Street.** George Washington built a town house on this very spot, including a stable and other necessary buildings, where he often stayed when visiting town prior to the Revolutionary War. While that house has been demolished, the current dwelling was built based on a contemporary drawing, and some believe that Washington's kitchen was incorporated into the nearby house at 506 Cameron, dating from 1817.

134 N. Royal St., Alexandria • tel 703-746-4242 • gadsbystavern.org
• $$ • museum by guided tour only; closed Mon.–Tues. Nov.–March
• Metro: King St.–Old Town

Lee-Fendall House

4 Lawyer Philip Fendall, cousin of Gen. "Light Horse Harry" Lee and husband of a distant aunt of Robert E. Lee, built this wood-frame house in 1785—the first of 37 Lees to reside here over the next 118 years. George Washington, one of Fendall's closest friends, dined here at least seven times. It's believed that Light Horse Harry Lee, who spent a great deal of time with the Fendalls, wrote his moving eulogy to George Washington here, penning the famous words describing the great man: "first in war, first in peace, and first in the hearts of his countrymen." Confederate general Robert E. Lee grew up across the street and no doubt stopped by to visit his cousins here as well.

Robert E. Lee, legendary general of the Confederate Army

The only way to see inside the house today is by guided tour, offered at the top of the hour; it takes you through the various rooms, furnished in the Victorian style of the 1850s through 1870s and showcasing family portraits, letters, and books. Keep an eye out for period pieces by local manufacturers. The fiery United Mine Workers leader John L. Lewis was the final resident of the home, between 1937 and 1969, and an interesting exhibit in one of the rooms honors him.

Even if you don't have time for a tour, you are free to relax—and even eat your picnic lunch—in the award-winning garden, with its towering magnolia and chestnut trees. From here you can also see how the house's vernacular "telescopic" architectural style works—the building is actually composed of several sections, each piece progressively smaller than the last; the Gothic Revival and Italianate flourishes were added later.

614 Oronoco St., Alexandria • tel 703-548-1789 • leefendallhouse.org • by guided tour only; closed Mon.–Tues. • $ • Metro: King St.–Old Town

Christge Church

5 See pp. 170–171.

118 N. Washington St., Alexandria • tel 703-549-1450
• historicchristchurch.org • Metro: King St.–Old Town

George Washington Masonic National Memorial

6 Rising 333 feet (101 m) on the hill at the head of King Street, the Masonic Temple, as it's called locally, is dedicated to George Washington, first president of the United States and the first of 14 U.S. presidents to be Masons. The Freemasons—a secretive fraternal organization that began in the 16th or 17th century within Scotland's stonemason guilds—built the ten-story shrine in the 1920s. They fashioned it after the Alexandria Lighthouse in Egypt to symbolize Washington's role as the guiding light of the American Republic, as well as to spread the "light and knowledge of Freemasonry to the world." Fans of the film *National Treasure* especially will appreciate the eclectic collection of artifacts found within. The one-hour tour lingers a bit on Masonic history, but it is worthwhile for the good collection of Washington memorabilia, including his family Bible, leather field trunk, and Clock of Death (the pocket watch stopped by Washington's physician at the moment of his death). The tools the doctor used to bleed Washington to death are also on display. The **Knights Templar Chapel** on the eighth floor is designed in medieval French Gothic style, with four beautiful stained-glass windows and an exquisite hand-crafted copy of the **Ark of the Covenant** inside a fake treasure room. From the open-air **observation deck** on the top of the tower (reached by elevator—which ascends at a 7-degree angle), all of Alexandria and beyond sprawls before your eyes. Be sure to take a look at the Masonic square-and-compass symbol on the lawn far below.

GOOD **EATS**

■ **ASHLAR RESTAURANT & BAR**
Mid-Atlantic fare in a beautifully restored federal-era edifice. **116 S. Alfred St., Alexandria, tel 703-838-8000, $$$$**

■ **BILBO BAGGINS GLOBAL RESTAURANT**
An American menu in a family-owned, casual setting. **208 Queen St., Alexandria, tel 703-683-0300, $$**

■ **THE FISH MARKET**
Chesapeake-style seafood in a historic warehouse. **105 King St., Alexandria, tel 703-836-5676, $$**

The view from the George Washington Masonic National Memorial

As you stroll back down King Street, make a detour south on Payne Street to Duke Street and the illuminating **Freedom House Museum** (*1315 Duke St., tel 703-836-2858, closed weekends*), which once held the nation's largest slave-trading business. Exhibits by the Northern Virginia Urban League remember the thousands who passed through—including Solomon Northrup, known for his memoir *Twelve Years A Slave*. If you don't want to walk the mile-plus (2 km) to the memorial from Washington Street, it's an easy drive; or you can hop aboard the free King Street Trolley, which runs every 10 minutes between the King Street–Old Town Metro station and Union Street.

101 Callahan Dr., Alexandria • tel 703-683-2007 • gwmemorial.org • tours daily at 9:30 a.m., 11 a.m., 1 p.m., 2:30 p.m., & 4 p.m. • $$$ • Metro: King St.–Old Town

Lyceum, Alexandria's History Museum

7 Take a stroll through Alexandria's past in this small museum, with exhibits telling the story of the city's original Native American settlements, its days as a colonial powerhouse and one of America's busiest ports, and the Civil War period in which it became the longest surrendered Confederate city (when the building itself served as a hospital). Artifacts, old photographs, maps, and original artwork add to the experience. A group of local Alexandrians founded the Lyceum in 1838 as an educational and cultural center.

201 S. Washington St. • tel 703-746-4994 • alexandriava.gov • $
• Metro: King St.–Old Town

Stabler-Leadbeater Apothecary Museum

8 George Washington, James Monroe, and Robert E. Lee all knew this family-run pharmacy, which operated between 1792 and 1933 and offered everything from tinctures to elixirs to cleaning products to paints to groceries. During the Civil War, when Alexandria was occupied by Union troops, soldiers stood in line here to purchase "hot drops," a cough medication containing paprika and alcohol. Preserved intact, the shop contains original potions, herbs, mortars, and journals. Look for the plaque showing the exact spot

Potions and powders from the Stabler-Leadbeater Apothecary kept generations healthy.

where Robert E. Lee was standing when he received the orders to put down the uprising at Harper's Ferry. Upstairs, the dark and musky, Harry Potter–esque manufacturing room, complete with wooden drawers labeled with such curious ingredients as Dragon's Blood and Gum Gambir, is where medicines were mixed and crushed. Visits by guided tour.

105–107 S. Fairfax St., Alexandria • tel 703-746-3852 • apothecarymuseum.org • by guided tour only; closed Mon.–Tues. Nov.–March • $$ • Metro: King St.–Old Town

SAVVY **TRAVELER**

George Washington lived (and died) at **Mount Vernon** (*mountvernon.org*), a plantation about 10 miles (16 km) south of Alexandria. Today it offers a fascinating glimpse into the life and times of the first president, with exhibits, tours of his home, gardens, and farm, plus breathtaking views over the Potomac. If you don't have a car, you can travel by boat cruise (*potomacriverboatco.com*). Another option is to bike to the estate along the riverside Mount Vernon Trail, then take a boat back to Alexandria (*bikeandrolldc.com*).

Torpedo Factory Art Center

9 Situated along the Potomac River, this former factory—yes, it actually made torpedoes—now contains 80-odd studios where you can watch local artists sculpt, paint, weave, and make stained glass (and buy their wares). Built in 1918, the factory turned out torpedo shell casings and other weaponry for both World Wars (look for the Mark XIV torpedo on view in the main hall, produced here in 1945). The federal government used the spacious building for storage until the city bought it in 1969. The art center opened in 1974, and it was incorporated into a waterfront development a decade later. The **Alexandria Archaeology Museum** on the third floor displays local artifacts (*tel 703-746-4399, alexandriava.gov, closed Mon.*).

Out back, amble along the boat docks, enjoy a meal at a nearby restaurant, or park yourself on a bench and take in the fresh air, along with musicians and other entertainers. Here, too, you can pick up a **water taxi** to the new National Harbor development across the river, to a Nationals baseball game, or for a spin around the monuments, among other options (*potomacriverboatco.com*).

105 N. Union St., Alexandria • tel 703-838-4565 • torpedofactory.org • Metro: King St.–Old Town

Christ Church

Many of America's forefathers worshipped at this colonial-era church.

The serene sanctuary of Christ Church; the wineglass pulpit dates from an 1890s restoration.

Built in the style of an English country church before the city of Alexandria was even established, Christ Church remains a bucolic oasis—and an active church—in the heart of the bustling city. Designed by James Wren and completed in 1773, it features a brick exterior and whitewashed interior. Its greatest claim to fame, however, is the fact that George Washington worshipped here, as did Robert E. Lee. Docents lead tours daily; meet at the church's front door.

■ MAIN CHURCH

Entering this bright space, you are immediately drawn in by the Palladian chancel window in front, unusual for its time. Note the cut-glass chandelier under the west gallery, advanced lighting in the early 1800s. George Washington was one of the first to purchase a box pew, now marked by a silver plaque (**No. 60**). The story goes that it was on the church's lawn that he declared his intent to fight the Revolutionary War. Robert E. Lee attended services here with his family from the age of three; a silver plaque on the chancel commemorates his confirmation here in 1853.

■ CHURCHYARD

Many of Alexandria's earliest residents were buried in the churchyard. By 1809, however, most burials were banned for sanitation and space concerns. Take a stroll around, reading the faint tombstones (although the gravestones that exist today are originals, they're not necessarily placed on their original spots; during the Civil War, Union soldiers stacked them against the Parish House and all order was lost). Among those laid to rest here are the city founder, Lord Mayor William Ramsay, and his wife, as well as Col. Philip Marsteller, one of George Washington's pallbearers (though his table stone monument was carted off during the Civil War). An unpretentious ivy-covered mound near Washington Street is the final resting place for Confederate prisoners of war.

■ MUSEUM

The **Memorial Parish House** maintains a small historic display, where plaques reveal more history about the church and its people through the centuries.

SAVVY **TRAVELER**

Old Town is filled with other early American churches, including:

Alfred Street Baptist Church (301 S. Alfred St.) Founded by slaves in 1803.

Old Presbyterian Meeting House (316 S. Royal St.) Dating from 1774.

St. Mary Catholic Church (310 S. Royal St.) Virginia's oldest Catholic church, founded in 1775.

St. Paul's Episcopal Church (228 S. Pitt St.) Benjamin Latrobe's only surviving Gothic Revival–style structure, dating from 1817.

OLD TOWN ALEXANDRIA

118 N. Washington St., Alexandria • tel 703-549-1450 • historicchristchurch.org • Metro: King St.– Old Town

Colonial Alexandria

In the 18th century, Alexandria thrived as a key port city in the colony of Virginia. Against a backdrop of early settlement and revolutionary turmoil, daily life went on in taverns, riverfront businesses, and churches—with much debate about the growing British "situation." Today much of the colonial essence remains in brick and clapboard town houses, cobbled streets, and pocket gardens, while house museums give a sense of life at the start of America. Some typical characteristics:

Above: Block after block of unbroken rows of narrow houses, their front doors opening to the street, add to Old Town Alexandria's charm. Opposite: Carlyle House, built in 1752, hosts many special events recalling the colonial era.

Architecture
Alexandria's earliest houses were built in the symmetrical Georgian style, with its classic proportions and ornamental elements. Beginning around 1780, the most prevalent style of architecture found here was named after its era, the federal period, and featured plainer surfaces and isolated detail.

Decor
The colonial-era elite looked to Europe for their furnishings and adornments, including hand-printed wallpaper, finely woven rugs, and ornate wood furniture made by skilled craftsmen. Those who couldn't afford such extravagance cobbled together what they could—homespun fabrics for curtains; braided, hand-woven, or hooked rugs; furniture made by local villagers, or the homeowners themselves. Common themes included the pineapple (symbol for hospitality), weeping willow (longevity), heart (love), and anchor (hope). Patterns such as stripes, plaids, and checks were also common.

Gardens

At a time when England was turning toward natural-istic gardens, the American colonists preferred the more conservative Anglo Dutch style—geometric symmetry within an enclosed space. Gardens, nor-mally planted behind the house in the urban centers due to space constraints, served to provide produce for the table, as well as beauty pleasing to the eye.

Churches

Church steeples spangled the colonial-era skyline. The Anglican church, or Church of England, was the established religion of Virginia, and Sunday services provided a social outlet. Attendance and taxes were mandatory by law. Little by little, other religions took hold, including Presbyterians, Methodists, Baptists, and Quakers— adding fuel to the fire of revolution, in a young land yearning for personal freedoms.

EARLY **HOMES**

Old Town Alexandria, along with Georgetown, is filled with edifices built at the time of the Revolutionary War. Some buildings are open to visitors as museums, others remain private. All provide a glimpse back into the nation's earliest days.

Captain's Row (late 18th c) Prince St. bet. S. Fairfax St. & S. Lee St., Alexandria, VA

Carlyle House (1752) 121 N. Fairfax St., Alexandria, VA

Old Stone House (1765) 3051 M St., N.W., Georgetown

Ramsay House (1724) 221 King St., Alexandria, VA

River Farm (1757) 7931 E. Boulevard Dr., Alexandria, VA

Living History

Meet George Washington himself at Mount Vernon—then speak to a tenant farmer at a nearby farm to learn what life was like for other colonial-era Virginians. (Hint: They did not all live in multiroom mansions.) The greater Washington area is full of historic sights offering a chance to interact with historical figures—soldiers, doctors, farmers, innkeepers, and more—and experience where and how they lived. Here are some of the best.

OLD TOWN ALEXANDRIA

■ GADSBY'S TAVERN MUSEUM
Take tea with Martha Washington at the annual Ladies Tea, or join Gen. George Washington at the annual **Birthnight Banquet and Ball,** set in the year 1799 (period attire optional). Costumed interpreters lead daily tours and an after-hours candlelight tour.

134 N. Royal St., Alexandria • tel 703-746-4242 • gadsbystavern.org • $$–$$$$$ • Metro: King St.– Old Town

■ STABLER-LEADBEATER APOTHECARY MUSEUM
Watch reenactors conduct authentic 18th-century scientific experiments in this historic apothecary in Old Town Alexandria.

105–107 S. Fairfax St., Alexandria • tel 703-746-3852 • apothecarymuseum.org • closed Mon.– Tues. Nov.–March • $$ • Metro: King St.–Old Town

■ CARLYLE HOUSE HISTORIC PARK
Meet members of the First Virginia Regiment at the **Annual Soldier's Christmas Open House Event,** just one of various reenactments that take place throughout the year at this historic manse in the heart of Old Town Alexandria. **John Carlyle's 1780 Funeral Reenactment** is another popular event.

121 N. Fairfax St., Alexandria • tel 703-549-2967 • nvrpa.org • $ • closed Mon. • Metro: King St.– Old Town

■ MOUNT VERNON
George Washington considered himself a farmer first and foremost, and, when he wasn't fighting wars or running the country, he devoted himself to improving American agriculture at his Mount Vernon plantation, about 10 miles (16 km) south of Alexandria.

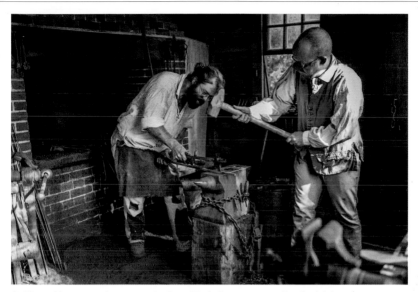

At Mount Vernon, tradesmen use tools and techniques common in colonial times.

Today, watch costumed interpreters demonstrate 18th-century agricultural methods and discuss events and issues of the day at the 16-sided treading barn (invented by Washington), slave cabin, and pole shelter. Other special events throughout the year include **Washington's birthday** (attended by the great general himself) and **Christmas at Mount Vernon,** when the plantation is decked out with colonial trimmings.

3200 Mount Vernon Memorial Highway, Mount Vernon • tel 703-780-2000 • mountvernon.org • $$$$ • Metro: Huntington, then Fairfax Connector Bus #101; see sidebar p. 169.

■ FORT WARD MUSEUM & HISTORIC SITE

Civil War–era soldiers and civilians reenact military life at this former Union Army installation built to defend Washington, D.C., during the Civil War—including infantry drills, artillery, camp life, and more. You'll talk firsthand to such famous people as Walt Whitman and Clara Barton, as well as surgeons, laundresses, engineers, and others.

4301 West Braddock Rd., Alexandria • tel 703-746-4848 • closed Mon. • alexandriava.gov • Metro: King St.–Old Town, then AT5 DASH bus to Landmark

Court of Neptune Fountain,
Library of Congress

PART 3

Travel Essentials

PLANNING YOUR TRIP

When to Go

April to May and September to November are the loveliest times to visit Washington, with generally comfortable temperatures and spectacular foliage—whether it's colorful blossoms or changing leaves. The busy tourism season starts in April with families and students on spring break. The cherry blossoms typically bloom around the Tidal Basin in late March or early April (see pp. 64–65); don't be surprised if it's still chilly at this time. July and August are hot and steamy, though many museums blast their air conditioners enough to warrant a light jacket. Winter is the low season, with modest snowstorms and freezing temperatures; when it does snow, streets may not be cleared immediately.

Rain is fairly evenly divided throughout the year (an average of 3.31 inches (8.4 cm) per month), except for afternoon thundershowers in June, July, and August.

What to Bring

Dress for the season and keep an umbrella handy. Heavy winter coats are usually essential December through February, and bring a light coat or jacket for the cooler spring or fall months (and even in summer for those air-conditioned museums). A hat in summer can help ward off the sun. Comfortable walking shoes are a given year-round.

VISITOR INFORMATION

The best source of visitor information is Destination D.C. (washington.org), Washington's official tourism site. It publishes a free visitors guide twice a year with comprehensive listings of attractions and events. Order or download it online.

NEGOTIATING THE CITY

When seeking a sight, first check the quadrant address, which indicates where it lies vis-à-vis the Capitol. Are you looking for N.W., N.E., S.W., or S.E.? The city is laid out in these four quadrants (see sidebar p. 9), with the Capitol building in the center. North Capitol, South Capitol, and East Capitol Streets radiate from this nucleus, separating the quadrants (the Mall runs west from the Capitol building).

Be advised that many District addresses can be found in more than one quadrant (for instance, there can be a 4000 M St. in N.E., S.E., S.W., and N.W.—four different D.C. locations).

After locating the quadrant, note that there are three types of streets in Washington. First are the numbered streets, running in a north–south direction from the Capitol. First Street, for instance, is located one block east or west of North or South Capitol Street, respectively.

The second street type is the lettered or named streets laid out in an east–west direction. Starting from East Capitol Street or the Mall, the streets run through the alphabet (with the exceptions of J, X, Y, and Z). The ones nearest the Capitol are one-syllable words; when the alphabet has been run through, they become two syllables, then three. As such, you can tell how far a certain street is from the Capitol by the letter with which it begins and how many syllables it contains.

Finally, the avenues that are named after states run diagonally across the grid.

SECURITY

Security has become a major issue in many places worldwide, but it is especially a concern in and around Washington's public areas and government buildings. Streets are sometimes closed down with or without notice, and may be blocked off by concrete barriers.

Metal detectors are standard equipment in most public buildings. Be prepared to have your belongings scanned and searched. If you have a pacemaker or other medical device that might be affected, let the guards know. And do not carry anything that could be considered a weapon and might be confiscated—for example, Grandpa's treasured pocketknife.

HOW TO GET TO WASHINGTON, D.C.

By Airplane

Washington, D.C., is served by three major airports: The closest is Ronald Reagan Washington National Airport (DCA) in Virginia, about 4 miles (6 km) from the city center; Washington Dulles International Airport (IAD), is 25 miles (40 km) west of Washington; and Baltimore–Washington International Thurgood Marshall Airport (BWI) stretches 25 miles (40 km) northeast of Washington, in Maryland.

DCA (known locally as "Reagan" or "National") is the closest airport to the city and also the most convenient. Washington's Metro system has a station right there. Taxi fare downtown is about $20. IAD (called "Dulles") is served by its own Washington Flyer taxi fleet (*tel 888-927-4359, washfly.com*), with 24-hour service to and from the airport. Taxi fare to downtown Washington from Dulles is about $60. Washington Flyer also operates coach service (*tel 888-WASHFLY*) connecting Dulles to the Wiehle–Reston East Metro station for about $5 one way.

The best way to get to and from BWI Airport is by train. Both MARC's Penn Line (*tel 800-325-RAIL, weekdays only*) and Amtrak (*tel 800-872-7245, must buy ticket for specific train*) provide frequent service between Union Station on Capitol Hill and BWI's own rail station; a free shuttlebus

connects the rail station and the airport terminal. Taxis between BWI and downtown D.C. cost about $90.

Airport Information

For general airport information: Reagan National (*tel 703-417-8000*), Dulles (*tel 703-572-2700*), and BWI (*tel 410-859-7100, bwiairport.com*); Dulles and Reagan share a website (*metwashairports.com*).

By Train

Amtrak trains arrive at Washington's Union Station on Capitol Hill. The station, which has shops, restaurants, and a food court, is worth a visit for its own sake (see p. 72). Although locals use the train mostly as a fast, convenient way to get to New York on the Acela and Northeast Regional trains, Washington is a major rail hub, connecting the capital by train to most U.S. destinations with rail service. The Metro station at Union Station provides easy access to the rest of the city and beyond.

Amtrak information: *tel 800-872-7245, amtrak.com*

GETTING AROUND

By Metro

The Washington Metropolitan Area Transit Authority operates the bus and subway systems in the metropolitan area. Metrorail stations are clearly marked by large columns with brown "M" signs.

The clean and efficient rail network makes it very

easy to get around the region, but maintenance and repairs required from the growing number of riders means there may be occasional delays or outages on some sections of the system. In such cases bus transfer between stations is usually available. Metro posts regular updates about operating status (*wmata.com*). Most suburban stations have lots for all-day parking, but go early because they fill up fast.

Fares range from roughly $1.70 to $5.90 one way, based on distance and time of day. You must purchase a plastic, rechargeable SmarTrip card, available online, at any Metrorail station, at CVS pharmacies in the D.C. area, and at other retail outlets. Fare information is available near the ticket machines.

Metrorail opens at 5 a.m. on weekdays and 7 a.m. on weekends. It closes at midnight Sunday through Thursday. On Friday and Saturday nights, it runs until 3 a.m.

Metro route information: *tel 202-637-7000, wmata.com*

By Bus

Metrobus service covers the city and the suburbs, with some lines running 24 hours. The fare for any destination within Washington is $1.75, or $4.00 for express service. Exact fare is required. For route and fare information, *tel 202-637-7000, wmata.com*. For just $1 per ride, the DC Circulator bus service operates daily in central Washington, with frequent stops. The five routes extend from Dupont Circle to Rosslyn; Georgetown to Union Station; Union Station to Navy Yard; Woodley Park to McPherson Square; Potomac Avenue to Skyland; and around the National Mall. Visit *dccirculator.com* for route schedules and maps.

By Taxi

Cabs in Washington are plentiful and fairly inexpensive. It's usually possible to hail a cab on any major street. They run on a meter system, and there are surcharges for each extra passenger, rush hour, snow emergency, and baggage. Information on surcharges is posted in every cab.

By Bicycle

The popular bike-sharing program, Capital Bikeshare (*capitalbikeshare.com),* offers more than 3,000 bikes at more than 350 stations throughout the District as well as in nearby Arlington, Virginia; Alexandria, Virginia; and Montgomery County, Maryland. The distinctive bright-red bikes can be found at most Metro stations and at convenient locations downtown and along the National Mall. Regular users can buy a daily, monthly, or annual membership online, while visitors can use a credit card at any Bikeshare station kiosk to purchase a 24-hour pass for $7 or a 3-day pass for $15. Note that bike helmets, required by law for riders under age 16, are not available.

By Car

Visitors should consider the possibility that a car will be more of an annoyance than a convenience. Parking is difficult, and parking garages are expensive.

Should you find on-street parking, check the signs, since many streets become no-parking zones during rush hour. If your car is not where you left it, call *tel 202-541-6083* for information on its location.

Some streets are two-way most of the time, but during rush hour become one way—including Rock Creek and Potomac Parkways and 17th Street, N.W.

TRAVELERS WITH DISABILITIES

D.C. is a very accessible place for travelers with disabilities. The Washington Metropolitan Area Transit Authority also publishes a free pamphlet on Metro's bus and rail system accessibility for the elderly and physically disabled. Call *tel 202-962-1100* to order the guide, or visit Metro's website at *wmata.com.*

Smithsonian museum buildings are accessible to wheelchair visitors. Find detailed information online at *si.edu* or call *tel 202-633-2921.*

Government buildings are generally open to the public, but be advised that they may close for security reasons with little or no notice. Be flexible, and call ahead.

CRIME & EMERGENCIES

Crimes of all sorts have been on the decrease in the last few years in Washington, but precautions are advised.

Don't wander onto deserted or ill-lighted streets or parks, particularly at night. If you're uncomfortable in a neighborhood, leave.

If someone tries to rob you, give the robber whatever he or she asks. Remember, your life is more valuable than your belongings.

Emergency Numbers

In an emergency, call 911.

• Police/fire/ambulance: 911

• City Services and information (non-emergency): 311

• Metro Transit Police (emergency): 202-962-2121

• International Visitors Information Desk (offers multilingual information and assistance; located at Dulles): 703-572-2536

• Travelers Aid: 202-371-1937

• U.S. Park Police (emergency): 202-610-7500

Lost Credit Cards

American Express: 800-528-4800
Diners Club: 800-234-6377
Discover Card: 800-347-2683
MasterCard: 800-424-7787
Visa: 800-847-2911

HOTELS

When it comes to travel, where you sleep can make all the difference. Washington, a city that **hosts guests from all nations, offers a panoply of selections in all price categories and styles.**

Washington hotels vary from the luxurious and very expensive—the Four Seasons in Georgetown and the Mandarin Oriental near the National Mall included—to the basic and still fairly expensive, such as the large downtown hotels that cater mostly to the convention and meeting trade. Small and charming is harder to find, but the new boutique hotels opened by the Kimpton Group are a hopeful sign.

Because every major business in the country is affected by government legislation and regulations, Washington hotels cater to business travelers on expense accounts. That means high prices during the week, when businesses are paying the tab, with weekend bargains for leisure and family travelers.

Hotels in the city are expensive, so some visitors prefer to stay in less expensive places in suburban Virginia or Maryland and travel into the city each day. Many hotels routinely offer rates cheaper than their posted rack rates, and many properties offer discounts through organizations such as AAA or AARP. Note that most are nonsmoking establishments.

Organization

Hotels are listed by chapter area, then by price category, then alphabetically. Hotel restaurants of note are also included.

Price Range

An indication of the cost of a double room in the high season is given by **$** signs.

$$$$$	Over $225
$$$$	$175–$225
$$$	$125–$175
$$	$85–$125
$	Under $85

Text Symbols

- 🛈 *No. of Guest Rooms*
- 🅿 *Parking*
- 🛗 *Elevator*
- 🏊 *Outdoor Pool*
- 🏊 *Indoor Pool*
- 🏋 *Gym*
- 📶 *Wi-Fi*
- 💳 *Credit Cards*
- Ⓜ *Metro*

NATIONAL MALL

■ MANDARIN ORIENTAL
$$$$$
1330 MARYLAND AVE., S.W.
TEL 202-554-8588
**mandarinoriental.com/
washington**

This super-luxury hotel near the National Mall's southeastern end overlooks the Tidal Basin and the Jefferson Memorial. The marble baths, lacquered furniture, silk furnishings, and extensive spa services make for a soothing stay.

🛈 *400* 🅿 🏊 🏋 📶 *Free* 💳 *All major cards* Ⓜ *L'Enfant Plaza*

CAPITOL HILL

■ THE GEORGE
$$$$$
15 E ST., N.W.
**TEL 202-347-4200 OR
800-546-7866**
hotelgeorge.com

A completely renovated building (from 1928), the George is a Kimpton hotel with striking decor, convenient to Capitol Hill attractions. The restaurant **Bistro Bis** *(tel 202-661-2700)* offers quality contemporary French bistro fare.

🛈 *139* 🅿 🏋 📶 *Charge* 💳 *All major cards* Ⓜ *Union Station*

■ CAPITOL SKYLINE HOTEL
$$$$
10 I ST., S.W.
202-488-7500 OR 800-458-7500
capitolskyline.com

With a free shuttle to D.C.'s major sites, this seven-story downtown hotel is a celebration of modern design. The building itself is the masterwork of Morris Lapidus of Miami Beach fame, with furniture in the lobby by the likes of Frank Gehry, Eero Saarinen, and Philippe Starck. The decor of the large and light-filled guest rooms is a modern take on colonial style. While the hotel is perfectly safe, it is not necessarily advisable to walk in the surrounding neighborhood after dark.

🛈 *203* 🅿 🛗 🏊 🏋 📶 *Free* 💳 *All major cards* Ⓜ *Navy Yard*

HOTELS

■ **COURTYARD WASHINGTON CAPITOL HILL/NAVY YARD**
$$$$
140 L ST., S.E.
TEL 202-479–0027
marriott.com
A friendly staff and airy suites with refrigerators, microwaves, and wet bars add to the allure of this modern hotel located near a thriving neighborhood full of restaurants and bars—and a baseball's toss from Nationals Park—with a Metro nearby.
① *192 + 12 suites* **P** *Valet* ⬆ 🏊 📺 🛜 *Free* ⬥ *All major cards* 🚇 *Navy Yard–Ballpark*

■ **HYATT REGENCY WASHINGTON ON CAPITOL HILL**
$$$$
400 NEW JERSEY AVE., N.W.
TEL 202-737-1234 OR
800-223-1234
washingtonregency.hyatt.com
This large convention hotel with all the amenities occupies a full city block on Capitol Hill. Museums, monuments, and more are just steps away.
① *836* **P** 🏊 📺 🛜 *Free* ⬥ *All major cards* 🚇 *Union Station*

■ **LIAISON CAPITOL HILL HOTEL**
$$$$
415 NEW JERSEY AVE., N.W.
TEL 202-638-1616
jdvhotels.com
This boutique hotel, located between Union Station and Capitol Hill, features a rooftop bar, seasonal pool, and the **Art and Soul** restaurant *(tel 202-393-7777)*.
① *343* 🏊 📺 🛜 *Free* ⬥ *All major cards* 🚇 *Union Station*

■ **PHOENIX PARK HOTEL**
$$$$
520 N. CAPITOL ST., N.W.
TEL 202-638-6900 OR
877-237-2082
phoenixparkhotel.com
Named after a park in Dublin, this hotel has a European ambience. The adjoining **Dubliner Restaurant and Pub** *(tel 202-737-3773)* offers good pub cooking and Irish entertainment.
① *149* **P** 📺 🛜 *Free* ⬥ *All major cards* 🚇 *Union Station*

■ **WASHINGTON COURT HOTEL**
$$$$
525 NEW JERSEY AVE., N.W.
TEL 202-628-2100
washingtoncourthotel.com
This convenient, comfortable hotel has a dramatic four-story atrium lobby and billiards in the Federal City bar.
① *265* **P** 📺 🛜 *Free in public areas* ⬥ *All major cards* 🚇 *Union Station*

■ **CAPITOL HILL HOTEL**
$$$
200 C ST., S.E.
TEL 202-543-6000
capitolhillhotel-dc.com
Tucked behind the Library of Congress on the House side of the Hill, this hotel offers kitchenettes in every suite.
① *155* **P** 🛜 *Free* ⬥ *All major cards* 🚇 *Capitol South*

WHITE HOUSE & AROUND

■ **FAIRMONT HOTEL**
$$$$$
2401 M ST., N.W.

TEL 202-429-2400 OR
800-257-7544
fairmont.com/washington
Built around a courtyard, the Fairmont is in the West End area of town near Georgetown. Rooms are luxurious, service is attentive. The fitness center, with pool, is one of the city's most popular. **Juniper** *(tel 202-457-5020)* offers modern American regional cooking.
① *415* **P** 🏊 📺 🛜 *Free in public areas* ⬥ *All major cards* 🚇 *Foggy Bottom–GWU*

■ **THE HAY–ADAMS HOTEL**
$$$$$
800 16TH ST., N.W.
TEL 202-638-6600 OR
800-853-6807
hayadams.com
Built where President Lincoln's secretary John Hay and John Adams's grandson Henry Adams lived, the hotel is just across Lafayette Square from the White House. **The Lafayette** dining room *(tel 202-638-2570)* and guest rooms on the south side offer great views.
① *145* **P** 🛜 *Free* ⬥ *All major cards* 🚇 *Farragut West, McPherson Square*

■ **THE JEFFERSON**
$$$$$
1200 16TH ST., N.W.
TEL 202-448-2300
jeffersondc.com
Regarded by many as the Capital City's finest small hotel, the Jefferson showcases many touches inspired by the third president of the United States.
① *95* **P** 🛜 *Free* ⬥ *All major cards* 🚇 *Farragut West, Farragut North*

■ PARK HYATT

$$$$$
1201 24TH ST., N.W.
TEL 202-789-1234

parkwashington.hyatt.com

Three blocks from Georgetown, in D.C.'s West End, the Park Hyatt has a lobby decorated with an impressive collection of art plus large and luxurious rooms. Its **Blue Duck Tavern** *(tel 202-419-6755)* serves accomplished meals including a lavish weekend brunch.

🛏 216 🅿 📺 🛜 *Free* 🏊 *All major cards* Ⓜ *Foggy Bottom GWU*

■ RENAISSANCE MAYFLOWER HOTEL

$$$$$
1127 CONNECTICUT AVE., N.W.
TEL 202-347-3000 OR
800-228-7697

themayflowerhotel.com

Once home to many members of Congress, the Mayflower has been the site of many inaugural balls. The gracious lobby runs an entire city block.

🛏 657 🅿 📺 🛜 *Free in public areas* 🏊 *All major cards* Ⓜ *Farragut North*

■ SOFITEL LAFAYETTE SQUARE

$$$$$
806 15TH ST., N.W.
TEL 202-730-8800

sofitel.com

Set in an 1880s building near the White House, this hotel has a restrained elegance. Its restaurant, **Ici Urban Bistro** *(tel 202-730-8700)*, serves French cuisine. **Le Bar** lounge *(tel 202-730-8703)* is also popular.

🛏 237 🅿 📺 🛜 *Free* 🏊 *All major cards* Ⓜ *McPherson Square*

■ THE ST. REGIS

$$$$$
923 16TH ST., N.W.
TEL 202-638-2626 OR
888-627-8087

stregiswashingtondc.com

The posh St. Regis, located near the White House and museums, boasts fine plasterwork ceilings, antiques, and ornate chandeliers.

🛏 172 🅿 📺 🛜 *Free* 🏊 *All major cards* Ⓜ *Farragut North*

■ WILLARD INTERCONTINENTAL

$$$$$
1401 PENNSYLVANIA AVE., N.W.
TEL 202-628-9100 OR
866-487-2537

**washington.intercontinental
.com**

A Willard hotel has been on this site since 1850. Abraham Lincoln stayed here before his inauguration, and Julia Ward Howe wrote "The Battle Hymn of the Republic" here. The hotel has recently been luxuriously updated. Its **Café du Parc** *(tel 202-942-7000)* features French bistro cuisine and exquisite pastries.

🛏 335 🅿 📺 🛜 *Charge* 🏊 *All major cards* Ⓜ *Metro Center*

■ W WASHINGTON D.C.

$$$$
515 15TH ST., N.W.
TEL 202-661-2400

wwashingtondc.com

Italian Renaissance meets modern cool in this beautifully refurbished hotel boasting a Bliss spa and the rooftop **POV** bar *(tel 202-661-2400)*, with its fabulous views of D.C.

🛏 317 🛜 *Free* 🏊 *All major cards* Ⓜ *Metro Center*

■ GEORGE WASHINGTON UNIVERSITY INN

$$$–$$$$
824 NEW HAMPSHIRE AVE., N.W.
TEL 202-337–6620 OR
800-426–4455

gwuinn.com

This vintage hotel, with Georgetown and the National Mall within walking distance, has basic but spacious rooms decorated with a traditional Williamsburg theme. Some have kitchenettes.

🛏 64 + 31 suites 🅿 *Valet* 🍴 📺 🛜 *Free* 🏊 *All major cards* Ⓜ *Foggy Bottom–GWU*

■ HOTEL LOMBARDY

$$$
2019 PENNSYLVANIA AVE., N.W.
TEL 202-828–2600

hotellombardy.com

Conveniently located near the White House and the National Mall, this romantic boutique hotel occupies a 1926 art deco apartment building decorated with European antiques. Some guest rooms have a separate sitting area and wet bar.

🛏 110 + 21 suites 🅿 🍴 📺 🛜 *Free* 🏊 *All major cards* Ⓜ *Foggy Bottom–GWU*

DOWNTOWN

■ THE HAMILTON CROWNE PLAZA

$$$$$
1001 14TH ST., N.W.
TEL 202-682–0111 OR
877-270-1393

hamiltonhoteldc.com

This small art deco hotel offers guests an elegant lobby and small, rich-colored rooms with modern amenities. Its location in the heart of the business district, near the White House as well as the National Mall, can't be beat.

🛈 *301 rooms + 17 suites* 🅿 *$* ⬆ 🖥 📶 *Free* 💳 *All major cards* Ⓜ *McPherson Square*

■ HOTEL MONACO
$$$$$
700 F ST., N.W.
TEL 202-628-7177 OR
800-649-1202
monaco-dc.com
This luxury Kimpton boutique hotel is housed in the stately 1839 Tariff Building in Penn Quarter, within steps of the action of the Verizon Center, Washington Convention Center, and 7th Street arts scene. Distinctive rooms with 15-foot (5 m) ceilings feature neoclassical furnishings and vivid colors.

🛈 *183* 🅿 🖥 📶 *Charge* 💳 *All major cards* Ⓜ *Gallery Place–Chinatown*

■ THE DONOVAN
$$$$–$$$$$
1155 14TH ST., N.W.
TEL 202-737-1200 OR
888-550-0012
donovanhousehotel.com
A rooftop pool and bar, pod-shaped spiral showers, a purple-olive-and-white color scheme, and complimentary wine hour highlight this hip boutique hotel on Thompson Circle named after Wild Bill Donovan, the spymaster who founded the CIA.

🛈 *193 + 17 suites* 🅿 *Valet* ⬆ 🖥 📶 *Free* 💳 *All major cards* Ⓜ *McPherson Square, Mt. Vernon Sq 7th St–Convention Center*

■ HENLEY PARK HOTEL
$$$$
926 MASSACHUSETTS AVE., N.W.
TEL 202-638-5200 OR
800-222-8474
henleypark.com
A Tudor-style hotel in the tradition of Europe's finest inns is one of D.C.'s most charming. Dozens of gargoyles and lead windows grace its exterior.

🛈 *96* 🅿 🖥 📶 *Free* 💳 *All major cards* Ⓜ *Mount Vernon Sq 7th St–Convention Center, Gallery Place–Chinatown*

■ LOEWS MADISON
$$$$
1177 15TH ST., N.W.
TEL 202-862-1600 OR
855-235-6397
loewshotels.com/ madison-hotel
Cozy and noted for its attentive service, the Madison offers a great location for exploring D.C. sights as well as the Dupont Circle area.

🛈 *356* 🅿 🖥 📶 *Free* 💳 *All major cards* Ⓜ *McPherson Square*

■ MORRISON-CLARK INN
$$$$
1011 L ST., N.W.
TEL 202-898-1200 OR
800-332-7898
morrisonclark.com
This stately Victorian inn just off Massachusetts Avenue was built as two townhomes in 1864. A grand expansion into the church next door doubled the room count. Chefs of the **Morrison-Clark Restaurant** (*tel 202-989-1200*) have won many awards for their New American cuisine.

🛈 *114* 🅿 🖥 📶 *Free* 💳 *All major cards* Ⓜ *Mount Vernon Sq 7th St–Convention Center*

■ HOTEL HARRINGTON
$$$
436 11TH ST., N.W.
TEL 202-628-8140 OR
800-424-8532
hotel-harrington.com
Low prices, a prime location, and very plain, clean rooms make the Hotel Harrington popular with school groups and others on a tight budget.

🛈 *242* 📶 *Free* 💳 *All major cards* Ⓜ *Metro Center*

DUPONT CIRCLE & ADAMS MORGAN

■ EMBASSY CIRCLE GUEST HOUSE
$$$$$
2224 R ST., N.W.
TEL 202-232-7744
dcinns.com
Tucked away on a tree-shaded street on Embassy Circle, this genteel B&B occupies the former Taiwanese embassy. Each room is individually decorated with antiques, original artwork, and Persian carpets. The complimentary breakfast is served in the formal dining room, and a wine hour is offered each evening. It's located just steps from Dupont Circle, with easy Metro access.

🛈 *11 suites* 🅿 *Valet* ⬆ 📶 *Free* 💳 *All major cards* Ⓜ *Dupont Circle*

■ THE NORMANDY INN
$$$$$
2118 WYOMING AVE., N.W.
TEL 202-483-1350 OR
800-424-3729
thenormandydc.com
Though rooms are small, a cozy wine hour, free afternoon

tea and coffee (and fresh-baked cookies!), and attentive service entice guests to return time and again to this chic, European-style hotel. The small patio in back is charming. Located near Adams Morgan and Dupont Circle, with the major D.C. sights a short Metro hop away.

🛈 75 🅿 Valet ⬍ 🍴 📶 Free ✦ All major cards 🚇 Dupont Circle

■ PALOMAR HOTEL

$$$$$

2121 P ST., N.W.
TEL 202-448-1800 OR
877-866-3070

hotelpalomar-dc.com

Sophistication and personalized service are the hallmarks of this Kimpton hotel inspired by 1930s French moderne style. Exotic woods, bold art, and geometric touches abound in this hotel.

🛈 335 🅿 ⛲ 🍴 📶 Free ✦ All major cards 🚇 Dupont Circle

■ SWANN HOUSE

$$$$$

1808 NEW HAMPSHIRE AVE., N.W.
TEL 202-265-4414

swannhouse.com

Occupying an 1833 Dupont Circle mansion, this homey inn features nine stylishly decorated guest rooms, each one with a different theme, from lighthouse to French country. A sip of sherry in the sitting room is an especially nice touch. Dupont Circle and Adams Morgan restaurants are within easy reach.

🛈 9 🅿 ⛲ 📶 Free ✦ All major cards 🚇 Dupont Circle

■ CHURCHILL HOTEL

$$$$

1914 CONNECTICUT AVE., N.W.
TEL 202-797-2000 OR
800-424-2464

thechurchillhotel.com

Located just north of the vibrant Dupont Circle area, the Churchill offers a variety of suites and rooms with separate studies.

🛈 173 🅿 🍴 📶 Free ✦ All major cards 🚇 Dupont Circle

■ THE DUPONT CIRCLE HOTEL

$$$$

1500 NEW HAMPSHIRE AVE., N.W.
TEL 202-483-6000

doylecollection.com

Overlooking Dupont Circle, this spacious, elegant boutique hotel includes a Presidential Suite and 9,000 feet of meeting space. All rooms have mini bars and free bottled water.

🛈 309 🅿 🍴 📶 Free ✦ All major cards 🚇 Dupont Circle

■ THE FAIRFAX AT EMBASSY ROW

$$$$

2100 MASSACHUSETTS AVE., N.W.
TEL 202-293-2100 OR
855-559-8899

fairfaxwashingtondc.com

Formerly the Westin Embassy Row, the hotel dates from 1924 and has been for many years the residential hotel favored by members of Congress. Former Vice President Al Gore basically grew up here. Guest rooms are luxurious, as one would expect from a hotel on Massachusetts Avenue's Embassy Row.

🛈 259 🅿 🍴 📶 Free in public areas ✦ All major cards 🚇 Dupont Circle

■ HOTEL MADERA

$$$$

1310 NEW HAMPSHIRE AVE., N.W.
TEL 202-296-7600 OR
800-430-1202

hotelmadera.com

This pampering hideaway is like a sophisticated B&B tucked in a quiet location near downtown office buildings and embassies.

🛈 82 🅿 📶 Free ✦ All major cards 🚇 Dupont Circle

■ MASON & ROOK HOTEL

$$$$

1430 RHODE ISLAND AVE., N.W.
TEL 202-762-3100 OR
800-706-1202

masonandrookhotel.com

You'll feel as if you're visiting your urbanite friend's chic home at this boutique hotel—one with Frette linens, in-room yoga mats, and an evening wine hour. Boasting some of the city's largest guest rooms, it's located on a quiet road near trendy 14th Street.

🛈 178 🅿 Valet ⬍ ⛲ 🍴 📶 Charge ✦ All major cards 🚇 Dupont Circle

■ OMNI SHOREHAM HOTEL

$$$$

2500 CALVERT ST., N.W.
TEL 202-234-0700

omnishorehamhotel.com

Opened in 1930 on 11 landscaped acres (4.4 ha) near Rock Creek Park—with its jogging trails and paths—the Shoreham is popular with conventions and large events.

🛈 834 🍴 📶 Free in public areas ✦ All major cards 🚇 Woodley Park–Zoo–Adams Morgan

■ ROUGE

$$$$

1315 16TH ST., N.W.
TEL 202-232-8000 OR
800-738-1202

rougehotel.com

Quirky red accents—from Bloody Marys to wax lips—dominate this hip Kimpton hotel within walking distance of Dupont Circle.

(i) 137 🛏 ☎ Free 🗝 All major cards 🚇 Dupont Circle, McPherson Square

■ TOPAZ

$$$$

1733 N ST., N.W.
TEL 202-393-3000 OR
800-775-1202

topazhotel.com

This Kimpton boutique hotel promises "cosmic energy and good karma." Complimentary yoga mats are provided in every room, and you can even get an energy drink on your way out in the morning. The **Topaz Bar** (tel 202-393-3000) is open for meals and drinks.

(i) 99 🅿 ☎ Free 🗝 All major cards 🚇 Dupont Circle

■ TABARD INN

$$$

1739 N ST., N.W.
TEL 202-785-1277

tabardinn.com

This small hotel is beloved by those who consider it quaint and adore the Victorian clutter. Locals frequent the hotel's **restaurant** (tel 202-785-1277) which has a charming outdoor garden and imaginative food. The rooms vary widely in size, so look before you commit.

(i) 40 🅿 ☎ Free 🗝 All major cards 🚇 Dupont Circle

■ KALORAMA GUEST HOUSE

$$

2700 CATHEDRAL AVE., N.W.
TEL 202-588-8188

kaloramaguesthouse.com

Located near the zoo, this Woodley Park guesthouse offers B&B-style accommodation in the European tradition. This means some shared baths, as well as continental breakfast, afternoon lemonade, and sherry in the evening. The many repeat customers can help attest to its comfortable atmosphere.

(i) 19 ☎ Free 🗝 All major cards 🚇 Woodley Park–Zoo–Adams Morgan

GEORGETOWN

■ FOUR SEASONS HOTEL

$$$$$

2800 PENNSYLVANIA AVE., N.W.
TEL 202-342-0444

fourseasons.com/ washington

Located on the very eastern edge of Georgetown, this luxurious hotel provides its guests with a civilized home base for the rest of the city. On site, the **Seasons** restaurant (tel 202-342-0444), overlooking the C & O Canal, is a favorite power breakfast spot. Also popular, the welcoming and well-appointed three-level fitness center with an adjoining spa is one of the most opulent in town.

(i) 222 🅿 🏊 🛏 ☎ Free 🗝 All major cards 🚇 Foggy Bottom–GWU

■ THE GRAHAM GEORGETOWN

$$$$$

1075 THOMAS JEFFERSON ST., N.W.
TEL 855-351-1292

thegrahamgeorgetown.com

Named for one-time Georgetown neighborhood resident Alexander Graham Bell, this posh hotel includes such touches as pillow-top mattresses and l'Occitane bath amenities. It is located close to the historic C & O Canal and its scenic towpath. **The Observatory** (tel 202-337-0900) rooftop bar and lounge offers panoramic views of the Washington skyline.

(i) 57 ☎ Free 🗝 All major cards 🚇 Foggy Bottom–GWU

■ RITZ-CARLTON GEORGETOWN

$$$$$

3100 SOUTH ST., N.W.
TEL 202-912-4100

ritzcarlton.com

Built on the site of what was once a brick incinerator building, complete with a 130-foot-high (40 m) smokestack, this luxury hotel offers a soothing retreat overlooking the Potomac waterfront.

(i) 86 🅿 🛏 ☎ Free in public areas 🗝 All major cards 🚇 Foggy Bottom–GWU

■ THE WESTIN GEORGETOWN, WASHINGTON D.C.

$$$$$

2350 M ST., N.W.
TEL 202-429-0100

westin.com/washingtondc

This low-key hotel, located between Georgetown and the

White House, is known for its friendly, attentive service. Comfortable rooms and a great location offer good value for visitors to Washington.

🛏 267 🅿 Valet 🖥 📺 📶 Free in public areas 💳 All major cards 🚇 Foggy Bottom–GWU

■ THE GEORGETOWN INN
$$$$
1310 WISCONSIN AVE., N.W.
TEL 866-971-6618
georgetowninn.com
This classic redbrick hotel has colonial decor, large rooms, and marble bathrooms. It's also conveniently located for Georgetown shopping and entertainment.

🛏 96 🅿 📺 📶 Free in public areas 💳 All major cards 🚇 Foggy Bottom–GWU

OLD TOWN ALEXANDRIA

■ MORRISON HOUSE
$$$$$
116 S. ALFRED ST.
TEL 703-838-8000 OR
866-834-6628
morrisonhouse.com
Recently reopened after a multimillion-dollar renovation, this Kimpton hotel evokes the atmosphere of Old Alexandria. Guest rooms are tastefully furnished in federal-period reproductions. If your schedule allows, dinner is offered at the hotel's acclaimed **Ashlar** (tel 703-838-8000) restaurant on site.

🛏 45 🅿 📶 Charge 💳 All major cards 🚇 King Street–Old Town

■ HAMPTON INN OLD TOWN
$$$
1616 KING ST.
TEL 703-299-9900
hamptoninn.com
Located in the heart of historic Old Town and near the Metro, this well-run hotel combines comfort and value with convenience. You can walk to many restaurants in the area.

🛏 80 🖥 📺 📶 Free 💳 All major cards 🚇 King Street–Old Town

■ HILTON ALEXANDRIA OLD TOWN
$$$
1767 KING ST.
TEL 703-837-0440 OR
800-445-8667
hilton.com
Just steps from the Metro, convenient to Alexandria's charming Old Town, this upscale hotel has been recently renovated.

🛏 241 🅿 🖥 📺 📶 Free in public areas 💳 All major cards 🚇 King Street–Old Town

■ MONACO ALEXANDRIA
$$$
480 KING ST.
TEL 703-549-6080 OR
800-368-5047
monaco-alexandria.com
This centrally located boutique hotel by Kimpton features Civil War flourishes as part of its decor. A hosted wine hour and complimentary bikes are some of the extra touches that make it a favored destination.

🛏 241 🖥 📺 📶 Charge 💳 All major cards 🚇 King Street–Old Town

ARLINGTON

■ RITZ-CARLTON PENTAGON CITY
$$$$$
1250 S. HAYES ST.
TEL 703-415-5000
ritzcarlton.com
Part of the Fashion Centre mall, this hotel offers luxury with the added advantage of shopping. Modern American cuisine and a popular afternoon tea are served in the **Fyve Restaurant Lounge** (tel 703-412-2762).

🛏 366 🖥 📺 📶 Free in public areas 💳 All major cards 🚇 Pentagon City

■ CRYSTAL CITY MARRIOTT
$$$$
1999 JEFFERSON DAVIS HWY.
TEL 703-413-5500
marriott.com
Located a mile (1.6 km) from Reagan National Airport, this hotel connects to the Crystal City Metro stop, offering easy access to the memorials and Smithsonian museums.

🛏 343 🖥 📺 📶 Free in public areas 💳 All major cards 🚇 Crystal City

■ KEY BRIDGE MARRIOTT
$$$$
1401 LEE HWY.
TEL 703-524-6400
marriott.com
Just across from Georgetown, this hotel has easy access by Metro to downtown sites. **Capital View Ballroom** (tel 703-524-6400) offers an indulgent Sunday brunch.

🛏 582 🖥 📺 📶 Free in public areas 💳 All major cards 🚇 Rosslyn

INDEX

CREDITS

Author

Barbara Noe Kennedy

All photographs by Lisa A. Walker unless otherwise indicated below:

Picture Credits
**T = top, b = bottom,
l = left, r = right**

4 Randy Santos. **19r** Madonna and Child Enthroned With Four Saints, ca 1240/1245, Margaritone d'Arezzo, Samuel H. Kress Collection, Photograph © Board of Trustees, National Gallery of Art, Washington. **21** Cvandyke/Shutterstock. com. **22** Sam Kittner/Newseum. **25** Jeff Mauritzen. **26** Philip Gerlach/Gerlach Graphic. **27tl** Courtesy Clyde's Restaurant Group. **27b** Viktor1/Shutterstock. **28** Bill O'Leary/The *Washington Post* via Getty Images. **30l** Devin Murphy/Smithsonian's National Zoo. **36** Ricky Carioti/The *Washington Post* via Getty Images. **49** Chip Clark, Smithsonian Institution. **58** Marvin Joseph/The *Washington Post* via Getty Images. **63** Eric Long/National Air &

Space Museum/Smithsonian Institution. **67** U.S. Navy photo by Chief Musician Brian P. Bowman/Released. **78** f11photo/Shutterstock. **82** Harris & Ewing Collection/Library of Congress Prints and Photographs Division. **83** Universal History Archive/UIG via Getty Images. **89t** Tim Evanson, photo at www.flickr.com/photos/23165290@N00/8352478884, license at https://creativecommons.org/licenses/by-sa/2.0/legalcode. **89b** Olivier Douliery/Getty Images. **91** The *Washington Post*/Getty Images. **100** Abbie Rowe, White House/John F. Kennedy Presidential Library and Museum, Boston. **101** photo by Stan Barouh. **104** Kelly/Mooney Photography/Getty Images. **115** Richard T. Nowitz. **116** Paul Franklin/Alamy Stock Photo. **122** *Chicago Tribune*/Getty Images. **123** Abbie Rowe, White House/John F. Kennedy Presidential Library and Museum, Boston. **126** Randy Santos. **128b** ton koene/Alamy Stock Photo. **130** The *Washington Post*/Getty Images. **132** Courtesy of the President

Woodrow Wilson House. A Site of the National Trust for Historic Preservation, Washington, D.C. **141** Photo by Vivianne Peckham. **142** Danita Delimont/Alamy Stock Photo. **152** Charles Kogod/Getty Images. **154** Don Emmert/Getty Images. **157** Cvandyke/Shutterstock. com. **160t** Joseph Gidjunis, JPG Photography. **165** Everett Historical/Shutterstock. **167** MISHELLA/Shutterstock. **173** K. Rouleau/Carlyle House Historic Park.

Front cover Jefferson Memorial: Sean Pavone/Getty Images; Abraham Lincoln: David Evison/Shutterstock. **Spine:** American flag: M. Luevanos/Shutterstock. **Back Cover** Lisa A. Walker.

Created by Mary Norris Creative Services

Mary Luders Norris, *Editorial Director*
Marty Ittner, *Designer*
Maggie Smith, *Cartographer*

Since 1888, the National Geographic Society has funded more than 12,000 research, exploration, and preservation projects around the world. National Geographic Partners distributes a portion of the funds it receives from your purchase to National Geographic Society to support programs including the conservation of animals and their habitats.

National Geographic Partners
1145 17th Street NW
Washington, DC 20036-4688 USA

Become a member of National Geographic and activate your benefits today at natgeo.com/jointoday.

For information about special discounts for bulk purchases, please contact National Geographic Books Special Sales: specialsales@natgeo.com

For rights or permissions inquiries, please contact National Geographic Books Subsidiary Rights: bookrights@natgeo.com

The information in this book has been carefully checked and to the best of our knowledge is accurate. However, details are subject to change, and the National Geographic publisher cannot be responsible for such changes, or for errors or omissions. Assessments of sites, hotels, and restaurants are based on the author's subjective opinions, which do not necessarily reflect the publisher's opinion.

ISBN: 978-1-4262-1775-3

Printed in Hong Kong

16/THK/1

CREDITS